The Complete Guide

Creating and

Managing New Projects

for **Voluntary Organisations**

SECOND EDITION

Alan Lawrie

Published by:
Directory of Social Change
24 Stephenson Way
London NW1 2DP
Tel. 020 7209 5151; Fax 020 7391 4804
e-mail publications@dsc.org.uk
from whom further copies and a full publications list are available.

Directory of Social Change is a Registered Charity no. 800517

First published 1996
Second edition 2002
Reprinted 2006

ISBN-10 1 903991 15 3
ISBN-13 978 1 903991 15 2

British Library Cataloguing in Publication Data
A catalogue record for this book is available from the British Library

Cover design by Lenn Darroux
Text designed by Sarah Nicholson
Typeset by Tradespools, Frome
Printed and bound by Page Bros., Norwich

All other Directory of Social Change departments in London:
08450 77 77 07

Directory of Social Change Northern Office:
Federation House, Hope Street, Liverpool L1 9BW
Research 0151 708 0136

CONTENTS

FOREWORD TO THE SECOND EDITION

In the five years since the first edition projects have continued to dominate much of the life of voluntary and public agencies. Organisations are encouraged to bid for short-term project funding. New central, regional and local government initiatives are increasingly fixed-term. Long-term secure funding is rare. Organisations have to wrestle with short-term agendas, fixed-term funding and long-term needs and aspirations. At the same time funders are making increased demands for more detailed project plans, feasibility studies, exit strategies and monitoring.

This book aims to help managers be effective in designing and managing projects. It suggests practical strategies to deal with the work involved in planning, designing, managing, measuring and closing projects.

I am grateful to Jan Mellor, Peter Baker and Sandy Adirondack for their help in the first edition. I am also grateful to various clients and colleagues throughout the public and voluntary sectors whose ideas and experience developed my ideas and thinking.

Alan Lawrie
May 2002

Alan Lawrie is an independent management consultant specialising in organisational development.

INTRODUCTION

In an average year around 9,000 new charities are registered and 115,000 new commercial companies are formed. Throughout the economy new products and services are being introduced at an increasingly fast pace. Despite uncertainties concerning future funding and future prospects there is continual interest in creating organisations and projects.

This book looks at the key decisions and processes involved in starting up a successful project. It is relevant to two types:

- One set up as an entirely new and independent organisation with its own legal status.
- One created within an existing organisation. This could be a new service, a new activity or a new venture.

What is a project?

The-term 'project' is often used loosely. There are several different definitions of what is and what is not a project. Here are four of the most important features:

- **A project is unique.** There should be an idea behind a project that is new, different and innovative. It should not just be a copy of what has happened before.
- **A project is time limited.** Projects usually have a limited life. Often funding or other constraints limit their ability to become permanent organisations.
- **A project creates changes.** A project should have a clear plan of what it wants to change. There needs to be a vision behind the project. It should make some measurable difference. The changes should last after the project has gone.
- **A project is goal orientated.** A new project needs to have a realistic and achievable plan and strategy so that it makes the maximum impact. The way it is managed and organised needs to be goal orientated.

Sometimes projects lack these features or they are not fully developed. Often projects have them at the start but lose them as they become more concerned about internal issues and long-term survival. Projects can very easily stay past their 'shelf life'.

Projects can be independent or housed within organisations. Planning and managing them requires a different approach to many of the traditional ways of running a organisation. It also needs a willingness to adapt to new ideas.

Don't we have enough projects?

There is in the United Kingdom an abundance of charities, housing associations, statutory services, self-help groups, not-for-profit agencies and assorted quangos. In England and Wales more than 180,000 organisations are registered with the Charity Commission. So why spend time creating more new projects?

It can appear to be more effective to do something new. Often it seems easier to start something new – either inside or outside an organisation – than to try to change what an existing organisation is doing. Most of the discussion about managing change is about doing new things. The reality is often harder. Often organisational changes fail not because people do not want to do something new, but because they refuse to give up the old. Many organisational changes get blocked because it seems impossible to stop what you are doing and break with the past. A new organisation or project does not have the history and traditions that can hold a new idea back.

New projects travel lighter

Managed well, projects can create a new identity, build relationships, operate flexibly and work faster. In an established organisation it is easy for routines, structures and a sense of 'this is how we do it here' to get in the way. A new project can have a clear focus, and a vision and sense of direction that can unite and excite people. In an established organisation issues of vision, values and direction often become confused. The long-term survival of the organisation and the maintenance of the status quo becomes more important.

It is easier to sell a new project

For various reasons people who control resources often seem attracted to backing new projects rather than providing long-term support to existing ones. This can create a cynical atmosphere as applicants play a game with funders, automatically using words such as 'innovative' and 'creative' to repackage existing activities. Very few funders are willing to commit themselves to a long-term investment.

What makes a successful project?

There is no hard or reliable evidence about the success or failure of new projects in the not-for-profit sector. Evidence from various studies of small businesses suggests that as many as one in five will cease trading within two years of being established. Market forces can easily decide their viability. Not-for-profit agencies rarely have such a severe test. Success is much harder to define. If a charity fails to meet its objectives it is likely that it will struggle to continue until it either fades away or becomes moribund. In the public sector, if a statutory project or programme does not operate as intended, remedial action can often be late or non-existent. It is likely that the project will be quietly forgotten. Resources will be taken away from it to use in another project. A profit test is only appropriate for a commercial company. Many not-for-profit projects lack any measurable sense of success or failure.

In researching this book the most useful evidence was anecdotal. I was unable to discover the essential ingredients that would make any new project work. There is no foolproof guide on how to start a successful new project. Factors such as chance, serendipity, creative thinking and inspired leadership are often crucial. These factors are frustratingly difficult to package and replicate. It is possible, however, to describe the main tasks and processes involved and to suggest techniques and tools that can ease the process of starting up an internal and external process and make it creative.

Books that suggest simple formulae to guarantee success are dangerous because many of their case studies go through disasters and crises after publication. Today's stars often fall. There are two lessons from this. Firstly, success is usually only a temporary phenomenon and secondly, the critical factors that create success can often be lost along the way. However, in the research and discussions for this book, eight features kept cropping up as important issues in creating and managing the successful start-up of a new project.

A clarity of purpose

There is a strong sense of vision and values. People involved are focused on making a difference. They have a clear vision of what they want to achieve and the main steps towards the end result. Vision is the overall sense of what the project aims to do, change and achieve. It is about the big picture. Values are the ethos and principles that underpin the actions taken. Statements of vision and values need to be clear enough to unite people within the project and to explain the project to the outside world.

A sense of energy

There is a feeling of direction and even urgency around the project's activities and the work involved. People want the project to happen and are prepared to run an obstacle course to overcome barriers and hurdles. Project leaders need to be able to inspire confidence and communicate the project's vision and values.

Objective thinking

The people promoting the project regularly stand back and think through their assumptions about the project. They ask or have to answer searching and even awkward questions such as: will it really work? is it really that new? will it make a difference? They do not let their enthusiasm get in the way of dealing with hard issues.

Openness and participation

New people are welcome. Information is shared. Formal and informal networks of supporters, backers, friends and experts are formed to help get the project off the ground. Lots of people are encouraged to have a stake in it.

Teamwork

Often one or two individuals have a critical role in getting the project up and running. Without them nothing happens. However, they operate as catalysts by involving and supporting others. Few individuals have the talents, skills and patience to carry out all the tasks involved in starting a new project. People at the centre seem to operate as leaders and coaches rather than as sole performers.

Flexible working and management

Decision-making structures, budgets, job descriptions and organisational systems need to be clear, simple and capable of quickly responding to change. Any tendency to create bureaucracy and to add structures and overhead costs must be kept in check. New projects need to be able to make decisions quickly, act on them and move resources flexibly. Continual change and uncertainty is accepted as the norm.

A clear identity

New projects need to have an easily understandable identity and image. What it is for, what it will do (and not do) and what it values need to be presented in such a way that people can quickly understand and pick up the central message. People connected to the project should be able to describe its central ideas in headlines rather than having to write pages.

Exciting and challenging work

Often new projects get a sense of energy from the feeling that they are being creative and breaking new ground. Effective projects have an atmosphere and a style that is often dynamic, fast and informal. Some risks are allowed.

These features need managing. They do not just happen. They need leadership, organisation and teamwork. Starting a new project is hard work and often needs determination to see it through.

It is interesting to note that the issue of finance and available resources is absent from this list. It is not that they are not important, but they need to be seen in a proper perspective and considered at the right time. In a successful project the idea, the needs and the project vision are usually developed first. The search for cash and resources comes second. Trying to do it the other way round will often mean that the project becomes funder-led. All the ingenuity, ideas and energy behind it are suppressed to ensure that it fits the perceived interests and constraints of possible funders.

Two types of projects

One way of classifying new projects is to divide them into 'supply side' and 'demand side' projects.

A **supply side** project is developed because resources are available for a particular type of project. Money becomes available (often as a result of underspending at the end of the financial year) and project proposals are invited. The lead time in getting a project up and running has to be short. Usually the project has to be in place by a deadline. Mistakes can easily be made as things are done quickly

Some organisations have had difficulties in working with supply side projects. Often the project is finance-led. There is no time to test it out or consult with its users. At times all the emphasis is about getting the money spent before the end of the financial year. One organisation now keeps several project outlines 'on ice'. Should resources become available, it can quickly adapt the project to fit the relevant criteria.

Demand side projects are a result of people recognising new or existing needs or gaps in provision. Often someone with a view or a sense of vision is crucial in acting as a catalyst to get people to recognise a need and generate an idea to meet it. Demand side projects usually take longer to develop. Considerable work is needed to explain the project, win support and secure backing. Often demand side projects struggle to get access to funding.

No logical formula

Experience suggests that the life of a project does not follow a logical and tidy path. This book is designed around six main processes and groups of tasks. The steps are not usually neat and incremental, they are inclined to merge. Managing a new project requires coordination and organisation.

Encouraging innovation

There is little point in new projects simply copying what is already being done. It would be easier to extend or replicate what is already working than to go through everything involved in creating a new project. However, new ideas are often rare or discouraged. Innovation and creative thinking are often in short supply. They need to be encouraged, supported and managed.

Testing the idea

There are different ways of testing out an idea. Independent studies can be commissioned to research the idea's feasibility and viability. Pilots can be developed. It is also possible to run with the project and see if it works.

Building the case for the project

Before a project can be launched, other people will need to be involved and feel part of it. The essential idea and vision behind the project needs communicating and marketing. A network of alliances, backers and supporters needs to be built around the project.

Getting the project going

The project needs to develop momentum. There must be a strong sense of teamwork, one innovator is not usually enough. The project also needs to develop a plan to guide and monitor the start-up.

Designing the project

Projects need to be goal-centred, fast moving and able to use limited resources flexibly. Much traditional management practice and many organisational systems mitigate against this. Projects need to find ways of organising that support to enable them to meet rather than constrain their vision.

Getting the project organised

Detailed decisions about legal structures, finance and staffing will have a profound impact on the project. These issues must be planned and managed in a way that supports and enhances rather than restricting the project's strategy.

Four factors in a successful project

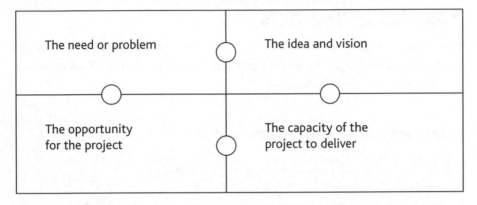

Successful project management is about connecting four different and sometimes conflicting factors:

The need

A project works best when the people involved in its development understand and appreciate why it is being proposed. It is important to evaluate the need or problem. What is its root cause? What are the symptoms? What is its scale?

The idea

Projects need a vision to unite their activities and efforts, from which strategies, objectives and workplans will flow. The idea behind the project should be clear enough to show how it will make a significant and sustainable difference to the need or problem.

The opportunity

Projects need to have or to create the space in which to operate. They must be actively supported and backed with more than just money. There must be support for the project from key people and a genuine commitment to see it through.

The capacity

Projects need to deliver the right balance of skills, energy, resources and organisation to get up and going and deliver results. They need to be designed to make an impact and create results.

All these factors need to be looked at and evaluated equally when designing a project. Too much focus on one or two factors can lead to others being ignored.

Four balancing acts

New project development can be difficult. Internal and external factors can easily be stacked against you. Four of the main issues most new project developers have to juggle with are described below.

Insecurity and short-term vision

One senior local authority manager commented that:

'Time spans have become shorter. We are under pressure to have things up and running much quicker. We need to see projects delivering much faster. Lead times have been cut. This is partly because we are often under pressure to spend money from central government and other funding programmes before a fixed deadline and also because our policy makers are increasingly impatient for change and seem regularly to change and alter priorities. For me long-term planning is about 18 months. I doubt that there are many people who could commit themselves to supporting a project financially for more than one year or two. Long-term and secure funding is unlikely to happen.'

This situation can easily cause insecurity and discourages long-term planning. It can also create a hand to mouth existence for projects, which live from one grant application to another. Consequently any long-term vision is lost or is shelved.

Security versus flexibility

At the start of a new venture it is impossible to be certain how things will work once it is up and running. What skills will be needed? What will the pattern of costs and income be? What issues will the project deal with? It is therefore logical to resist detailed planning and try to keep things flexible. However, funders often want to see stable and safe projects with detailed workplans and proper control systems. Staff understandably want secure terms and conditions of employment and a detailed job description. Managing the balance between stability and the need for flexibility and responsiveness is a difficult act in most organisations.

Fear of risk and wanting innovative solutions

In the private sector companies committed to new product research and development accept that many new ideas in which they invest time and money will never make it to market. This money will never produce a return on their investment. These companies have learnt to live with and indeed plan for failure. In the voluntary sector such a view is rare. Trustees are concerned about their legal responsibility as guardians of charitable money; funders express sharp concerns about wastage; managers are concerned about their credibility if projects do not succeed. However, the issue of risk and the potential for failure does need to be considered if an individual or organisation is to do anything beyond being safe, ordinary and predictable.

Balancing planning and doing

No feasibility study, market research report, cost benefit analysis or external consultancy report will guarantee a project's success. Often the only way of testing a project is by doing it. Many successful · projects were never properly planned, tested or piloted. The people behind them just set them up. They worked hard at ensuring that they succeeded. Such talk of bold innovation and social entrepreneurship usually overlooks a host of projects that did not deliver. Project failures are often conveniently forgotten. To win resources and manage risk, promoters of new projects increasingly have to demonstrate that their idea is properly tested, is needed and has been designed. You need to decide how much time to put into testing and designing the project and when to 'grasp the nettle' and launch it.

The project based organisation

Traditionally, organisations have been designed to be permanent, with fixed lines of accountability and clear allocation of responsibility, co-ordinated and controlled from the top down:

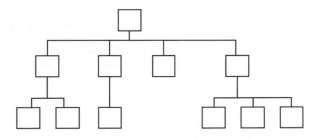

A project based organisation looks and operates differently. Everything is short term. Projects are forever starting and ending. The core of the organisation is continually developing new projects and initiatives which, in the main, are funded on a fixed-term basis:

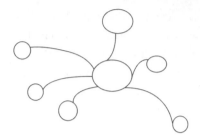

Surviving the project based organisation

The increased use of projects has several major organisational and management issues for organisations. Which of these do you recognise?

1   **How do you hold it all together?**
    When an organisation starts to operate as a collection of projects, someone needs to hold it together and ensure there is good communication between projects and between the centre and the core.

2   **Who funds the core?**
    Funders are often keen to fund or commission projects, but are sometimes reluctant to fund the organisation's core administration and central functions.

3   **Systems to manage flexibility**
    In a project-based organisation structures and systems need to emerge and be developed fast. The organisation's systems must be able to cope with short-term employment, the requirements of different funders and the ability to keep reorganising to take on new projects.

4   **Short-term funding – long-term planning**
    As funding becomes increasingly short term there is a need to keep the longer-term view. What happens after the project ends?

5   **Importance of innovation**
    Project-based organisations need to keep coming up with ideas for new projects and initiatives. They must be skilled at spotting new needs and opportunities.

6   **Need to learn and develop**
    The organisation must learn from each project. Systems must be developed that record and evaluate lessons that future projects can build on.

INNOVATION – ENCOURAGING AND DEVELOPING NEW IDEAS

This chapter looks at:

- What do we mean by innovation?
- Types of innovation
- The process of innovation

A truly innovative idea or project sounds like an exclusive, once in a lifetime event that can only be dreamt up by talented individuals with exceptional intelligence, creativity and imagination. In reality few organisations would seriously want to manage the process of having and developing ideas in such an idealistic way. There is little direct research into how voluntary or public sector organisations develop new services or activities, even though it seems almost mandatory to claim in annual reports, funding bids and publicity material that all work is innovative and ground breaking.

What do we mean by innovation?

There are very few original ideas. Most successful innovations are the result of adapting an existing idea or connecting a problem and a solution. Innovations are rarely huge initiatives. Innovation usually builds on what is happening already.

Many ideas happen accidentally or in the wrong place. One study by John Jewkes in *The Sources of Invention* (Jewkes et al, 1969) found that of 57 major inventions, ranging from ball point pens to engineering techniques, 48 were discovered whilst looking for something else or were invented by people who should have been doing something else with their time at work.

Often innovations happen despite an organisation's official management and decision-making systems, often in the shadows of the organisation.

One established project working with ex-offenders developed a new and successful system of peer support and group work without ever talking to anyone at the organisation's headquarters. Now, four years later, the scheme employs three staff and has an expanding network of volunteers. The project leader described the process of innovation that they adopted.

'We knew that if we asked for permission to introduce the new support system it would take ages. Papers would have to be written, reports commissioned and studies done. It would have left our hands and been taken over. Instead, we went ahead with it and quietly started piloting it. Once we knew that it was working we then introduced it to our senior managers in order to secure new funds for it. To their credit they supported it.'

Many new projects are started more by chance than by organised planning. Management writer Henry Mintzberg makes an interesting distinction between deliberate and emergent strategy in organisations (Mintzberg, 1994). A *deliberate* strategy is when managers clearly set out and plan for how they want their organisation to develop. An *emergent* strategy is when things happen as a result of chance, opportunity or even accident. Many organisations have invested heavily in commissioning research, designing blueprints and detailed budgeting only to find that their best-laid plans are out of date as soon as the ink is dry. Deliberate strategy is necessary. Without it total chaos would reign. However, too much deliberate strategy can make an organisation unresponsive and inflexible.

Deliberate strategy comes from	Emergent strategy comes from
Formal plans	Chance and accidents
The budget	People's pet projects
Workplans	Having the time to do something
External contracts and	different
commitments	Trying things out

A director of an arts centre describes how she struggles to manage the relationship between these two elements.

'By the nature of our work people are having ideas all the time. Several of our workers are very capable of getting involved in something by chance or working on what interests them. On balance it pays off, but it can be a bit chaotic. Most of our established and successful activities started out as a pet project of one or two staff. If

they want the idea to become a project they have to get backing for it. They have to navigate it into the formal side of the centre. They have to get a budget for it, get it programmed into our plans and get staff time to work on it. My job is to ensure a balance between the deliberate parts of the organisation (budgets, workplan, resources, business plans and contract obligations) and the emergent/chance activities.'

Just how innovative ...

In 1993 Stephen Osborne of the Aston Business School carried out a research project into the meaning and extent of innovation within voluntary organisations operating in the social welfare field. One hundred and ninety-five organisations from three areas took part in a survey. This was followed up by 24 in-depth case studies of individual organisations.

The findings raise the question of the actual extent of innovation within the voluntary sector:

- Forty-eight per cent reported no innovative developments.
- Of those that did identify some innovation, 26 per cent were of a developmental nature (the existing service is developed with the same client group) and 47 per cent described an evolutionary innovation (where new services are provided to an existing client group). Fifteen per cent reported expansionary innovation (using an existing service with a new client group) and 11 per cent identified total innovation (new services meeting the needs of a new client group).
- Very few organisations claimed innovations of national significance.

The report suggests that these findings 'refute the commonplace view of voluntary organisations as all inherently innovative'.

The follow up case studies also found no inherent characteristic of a voluntary organisation that could predispose it towards innovative activity. Rather the most significant factors were the expectations of key stakeholders within and without the organisation (particularly their major funders) and how it chose to respond to these.

Types of innovation

It is possible to identify three types of innovation.

A new activity, service or product

Finding a new way of meeting a need is a typical innovation. The voluntary sector has a track record in creating, sponsoring and setting up new projects to meet new needs. Community transport, citizens' advice bureaux and community businesses are all examples of initiatives put together to meet a need.

A new development in practice

Many innovations are concerned with developing different or improved ways of managing an existing problem or activity. This can include developing new processes or new techniques or using new technology.

A new strategy, direction or approach

Another type of innovation is the creation of an entirely different vision, values and direction for an organisation. Examples could include changing the basis of how an organisation works by giving greater control to users or by fundamentally changing the type of work. Sometimes this can only be achieved by creating a new organisation or distinct project.

The process of innovation

The innovative process can be described in five parts:

1   Creating an atmosphere that encourages new thinking.
2   Encouraging and supporting creative thinking.
3   Exploring possible sources of new ideas.
4   Managing innovation within the organisation.
5   Developing an idea into a proposal.

Creating an atmosphere that encourages new thinking

Fresh from an intensive (and expensive) residential management course, the director of a housing association called in his staff. He told them that they had his full support to think creatively, take risks and be innovative. After his pep talk experienced members of staff remembered their last experience of innovation. A new project had failed to live up to the original expectations. Despite considerable effort and commitment from the project leader results had been mixed and disappointing. The association had reacted by reducing the project's resources, gradually closing it down and reallocating the project leader to a boring and mundane job. He was a talented and intelligent individual who had thought it was understood that some risk was involved. He was now regarded as a failure. The association gave out a mixed message: 'Be creative and innovative' was the public slogan, but the hidden text said 'but, whatever you do... don't ever get anything less than 100% right'.

Creating an atmosphere that encourages people to question the status quo, look for better ways of doing things and come up with new ideas is not easy. A critical issue is stressing the importance of learning as a central feature of organisational life. Good learning creates an openness, inquisitiveness and curiosity that may lead to new insights and ideas. Several organisations are trying to develop the idea of a learning company that sees learning not just in a narrow sense such as attending external courses or job related training, but also encourages curiosity and long-term development and change. Learning is seen as a main building block of the organisation.

The following are examples of how we can create an atmosphere that encourages fresh thinking and innovation.

Encourage learning

Creating an organisation that encourages learning as a continual activity can lead to lots of new ideas. Learning does not only occur on training courses or in seminars. Effective learning can be organised in many different ways, for example mentors, secondments, distance learning, coaching and guided.

> One housing association is experimenting with the idea of giving each member of staff a minimum of five days' learning entitlement per year. They can use this time to attend formal courses, but many are now using it to evaluate existing services and develop ideas for new ones.

Encourage evaluation

Building in regular evaluation activities can be a way of encouraging new ideas. Evaluation techniques include surveys, review meetings, audits and discussion groups. Building regular evaluation into all aspects of the organisation's work can encourage innovation.

> An arts centre now holds a review conference after each event. The review has two parts: a 'post mortem' discussion looking at what did and didn't work and a 'what next' session to look at what has been learnt and to generate ideas for the future.

Encourage curiosity

Often in organisations working practices and processes fall into a routine. Things happen because they have always happened. The budget and the workplan are based on what happened last year. The organisation operates on 'automatic pilot'.

Encouraging people to ask why they do things is important and often challenging. Getting an organisation focused on work results and impact rather than its volume can be one way of encouraging fresh thinking.

Encourage feedback

Developing new ways of generating comments, reactions and complaints from the organisation's users, staff and other contacts can lead to several insights. Formal systems such as complaints procedures, satisfaction and review sheets are part of the process but are no substitute for 'walking the job' and being able to observe and listen to people.

Often even negative feedback, such as a complaint, can highlight how an activity can be improved, changed or enhanced.

Encourage flexibility

People need to see the wider context and the effect of what they are doing. Jobs and work are often compartmentalised and few people see the whole picture. Flexible working, job shadowing and job enlargement can help.

> An architects' practice changed how they managed projects. Staff were encouraged to manage a project from start to finish and to visit it regularly after its hand over. This small change (often called 'job enlargement') led to several improvements and better co-ordination of projects.

Encourage movement

Often people get stuck in a particular job. Their perspective of and involvement in their work becomes narrow. They lose a sense of vision and purpose. Some organisations encourage staff to move round projects, become multi-skilled and use appraisals and review meetings to chart their progress. Well planned and supported movements can help encourage an exchange of ideas and views.

Manage conflict

Often conflict is seen as wholly negative and to be discouraged at all costs. However, well managed conflict, focused on the problem and not the personalities involved, can spark off many insights and ideas. Getting different parties to a conflict to work together to define the issue, explore root causes and generate possible ways forward can provide new and valuable ideas.

Experiment with structures

New ways of working such as secondments, project or task groups and teamwork can lead to creative solutions. The structures should help people to look at things from a different point of view and develop new ideas.

> A national development agency has used project teams extensively over the past two years to develop key projects. Four or five staff from different functions work together on an issue for a short period and come up with a plan. Often the people with the least prior experience of the issue make the most valuable contribution. By asking obvious (or even seemingly idiotic) questions they challenge conventional practice and assumptions.

Get away from it all

Often you can be too close to a problem to think about it creatively. One company found that staff returning after short breaks, sabbaticals or transfers came back with a different insight to a long-term problem.

> One charity for people with learning difficulties holds an annual ideas day. All staff, board members and volunteers meet off site and must bring at least three new ideas to work on. The group works through each idea and develops a shortlist of ideas to implement on return.

Borrow from others

Some organisations have got the process of 'stealing' from others off to a fine art. It is important to keep in touch with developments in your field through professional bodies, networks and conferences. One project organises what it calls 'raiding parties', where staff visit similar organisations to look at how they operate and see what could be adapted in their project.

Encouraging and supporting creative thinking

Most ideas do not come from staring aimlessly at a blank sheet of paper in the hope that, like a flash of light, a new idea will burst forward. They are more likely to arise from a development of what you are already doing. We need to improve our skills to recognise the space for and ingredients of a new idea.

Will it work?

'Heavier than air flying machines are impossible.'

Lord Kelvin, President, Royal Society, 1895

'Everything that can be invented has been invented.'

Charles H Duell, Commissioner, United States Office of Patents, 1899

'We don't like their sound, and guitar music is on the way out.'

Decca Recording Co, rejecting the Beatles, 1962

Creative thinking techniques

Like any skill, creative thinking can be learnt and developed. Various techniques and models can be used to free up our thinking and encourage creativity.

Common blocks to creative thinking include:

- A tendency to conform.
- Fear of risk and failure.
- Failure to challenge conventions or assumptions.
- Polarising alternatives and choices.
- Fear of looking foolish.
- Working to rigid boundaries.

Some of the most common creative thinking techniques are:

Brainstorming

Brainstorming is a well established tool. It works on the basis that, from a wild or unusual idea something that is practical, creative and useful will emerge. There are three simple rules:

1 Pose a problem or question.
2 Generate and record as many ideas as possible.
3 Review ideas and build on possible solutions.

In the second stage it is important to go for as many ideas as possible. Participants should be encouraged to think freely and say whatever comes to mind. No criticism or discussion of anyone's idea should be allowed at this stage.

All ideas should be recorded on a common list so that in the third stage no one feels obliged to defend or justify their idea.

Lateral thinking

Edward de Bono developed the idea of looking at a problem both logically and laterally. Logical thinking follows a rational plan: the problem is defined, information is gathered, formal criteria for solving it are agreed, options are discussed and the most efficient option is selected. Logical thinking is useful and helpful. However, it can be restrictive and lead to predictable and unexciting solutions.

Lateral thinking is different. It places a much greater stress on challenging the problem, challenging any assumptions in the way the problem is posed and trying to turn the problem upside down. The central idea behind lateral thinking is to avoid moving directly from problem to solution. Instead it encourages you to search for an answer by looking at the situation differently. For example, a problem might not be a problem at all. A threat can at the same time be an opportunity. A strength can also be a weakness. Typical lateral thinking questions are:

- How can we look at this problem differently?
- How is it connected to other issues?
- What is the real problem?
- What is the root cause of the problem and what are the symptoms?
- How could the problem be turned into a solution?

Lateral thinking encourages you to think differently about the problem.

Six hat thinking

Edward de Bono went on to develop a 'six thinking hats' technique. His idea was that all individuals and groups can get stuck into a particular approach to looking at a problem. Individuals and groups should be able to wear all six hats in looking at an issue.

- **White hat thinking**. Deals in facts, known information. White is objective, neutral and unbiased. White is only interested in sharing information and establishing facts.
- **Red hat thinking**. The red hat is about feelings. It allows expressions of fear, excitement, passion, personal taste and intuition. It encourages hunches and 'gut reactions'.
- **Yellow hat thinking**. The yellow hat is all about being positive, constructive and making something work. It looks for the positive.

- **Green hat thinking**. This hat is all about being creative and encouraging the growth of new ideas, options and alternatives. It is concerned with fresh thinking.
- **Blue hat thinking**. Blue hat thinking encourages structures, logic and organisation in problem solving. It focuses on tidy and managed processes and decisions.
- **Black hat thinking**. The black hat thinking plays the devil's advocate. Black hat thinkers look for problems, risks and pitfalls.

Exploring possible sources of new ideas

New ideas can be developed in many different places. Here are four ways of discovering new ideas:

Taking a fresh look at what you are already doing

This can happen through formal processes such as commissioning an evaluation of what you do, carrying out surveys or comparing your work method with others in the same field. It can also happen accidentally.

> One environmental agency developed an entirely new way of working with schoolchildren as a result of some challenging questions asked by a newly appointed clerical worker. She thought that the way the schools programme was organised was out of date and unimaginative. After asking several 'awkward but painfully obvious questions' she persuaded the rest of the team to work with her to develop a new and very different project.

Challenging the way that you look at a problem

Often we get stuck into a predictable and routine way of thinking about a problem. We do not challenge or rethink our assumptions about it or ever look at the difference between the root causes and the symptoms of the problem. Trying to see an issue from a different perspective, thinking laterally rather than just logically or testing the validity of assumptions about the problem can all lead to a creative solution.

> A voluntary agency had debated for years what to do with its overcrowded and increasingly expensive city centre office. Various solutions were considered, such as moving, changing the office layout and building an extension. A session on creative thinking led to a different solution. At least half the staff were supposed to be working on

neighbourhood projects and did not need to be office based. The office was only ever overcrowded between 10 am and 4 pm and it was particularly overcrowded when field staff had to attend meetings, use the computers or attend supervision sessions. The agreed solution was that the central office needed to be smaller, with two satellite sub bases rented near to where the neighbourhood workers worked. Meetings and supervision sessions would be held at the sub bases. Field workers would be given laptop computers and be able to e-mail material to and from the main office. This solution created significant benefits. It reduced travel costs, reduced stress at the central office and, most importantly, refocused the organisation by shifting the physical presence from the city centre to the local neighbourhoods. By looking at the problem differently the agency discovered a useful and fruitful solution.

Adapting an existing solution to a new problem

Many innovations occur when something can be adapted from one use to another. All it requires is the capacity to make a connection between a need and a possible solution to a different problem. Much of the technology we use in our households started out life in industrial, commercial or specialist fields. For example, the TV remote control was originally designed as a niche specialist product for people with disabilities. It was not seen as having much mainstream potential.

Following up an opportunity

Many established organisations lack the capacity to identify new needs and encourage feedback from users. Such organisations are inward looking. They operate to a very narrow menu of what they can offer. A severe example of this was the manager of a local authority service who complained that members of the public kept phoning up his staff and 'asking for the wrong things'. Often organisations define themselves so tightly that opportunities are dismissed as not relevant.

Thinking and operating narrowly

A sports development project decided not to bid to a specification for a contract with their local health authority to develop a healthy lifestyle campaign. It felt that the project specification did not 'sound like us', although the actual work involved and the anticipated outputs and outcomes were almost identical to what they were currently doing. The specification was written in a health professional's rather than a sports development language.

Often people working in a particular sector or field make sense of it by developing their own language, practice and style. This is understandable, but can lead to a very narrow focus that can only relate to people who speak the same language. Narrow thinking often leads to a compartmental approach. Our starting point is what we do now and not what is needed. Creative thinking requires us to move away from our usual way of looking at or describing something.

We need to learn and innovate from what we already do. We need to develop a broader understanding of what is happening in the world outside and be willing to be flexible about how we can respond.

Often opportunities are missed as people are too busy dealing with day to day issues. Most organisations do what they are doing now as a result of history. They are driven by what they did last year. Keeping going and ensuring that existing expectations and commitments are met is often enough. The internal routine takes over. The main driving force is survival and ensuring that things continue from one month to the next. The organisation develops an atmosphere in which it is too busy to think, plan and respond to new opportunities.

Managing innovation within the organisation

Managing an organisation that genuinely supports and encourages innovation is hard. It involves undoing a whole way of operating and managing that has developed over time. But this process is necessary for innovation. The alternative is for managers to pay lip service to creating new activities but become frustrated as little happens.

Project development cycle time

In certain industries (in particular the car and computer industries) considerable effort has been made to cut down the time it takes to develop, design and produce a new product. The time involved in product development is known as the 'time to market'. New models of cars can now be designed, tested, engineered and produced in three to four years compared with the seven years it used to take. Many companies believe that their competitive edge will increasingly come from being first to the market with new and innovative products and services.

Organisations have invested heavily in streamlining new product development systems, in creating much more effective internal processes and in rewarding successful individuals and teams. Few not-for-profit agencies have the resources available to invest internally or reward success in financial terms. But it is interesting to see what (if any) internal processes manage the development of new projects.

Case study

A well-established organisation carried out a brief review, prompted by one individual commenting 'it took so long to get an idea agreed that it was not worth bothering with, as by the time approval was given it would be too late'. Three projects were used as case studies. Development time (the time from having the idea to the project being launched) ranged from nine months for a media campaign to three years for a local project. Despite 'innovation' being one of the main buzz words of the organisation's new mission statement, very little actually happened. New ideas had to run an obstacle course of meetings, reviews, planning sessions, budget cycles and detailed considerations. Many ideas got lost on the way. If an idea did get through, it was a wonder that there was anything left at the end of the process.

The review indicated four problems that frustrated new developments and suggested how they could be tackled:

- **No time**. The organisation operated at full capacity. Few individuals had time to think and discuss new ideas. The working style was all about being seen to be busy.
  Action: Responsibility for developing new ideas has to be seen as an explicit part of managing the organisation. Workplans, job descriptions, budgets and meeting agendas should have 'development' built into them.
- **No process**. People sponsoring a new idea had to navigate it through a plethora of meetings and committees. Responsibility for making a decision to back an idea was often avoided or put off. 'New ideas often hung around waiting for a green light.'
  Action: Responsibility for managing the process of project development and approval should be given to a senior person within the agency. The number of stages involved in getting project approval should be cut.
- **The present comes first**. Many people assumed that there was never any money for new ideas, so why bother having them? The main planning activity in the organisation was the annual budget. It should be the clearest statement of priorities. The starting point for putting the budget together was to cost in expenditure for current activities and projects. There was hardly ever any surplus income to use on new work. Many items in the budget were no longer priorities. They were there because of past decisions rather than current strategy.
  Action: The organisation should review all its activities and projects periodically and see how they fit with current direction and needs. It

should consider budgets for new projects at the same time as existing projects and activities.

■ **No resources**. The organisation did not have any financial resources to invest in new projects. Funders were perceived to be unwilling to allow them to develop any reserves.

Action: The organisation should build up a development fund equivalent to 4 per cent of its revenue. This fund should be used to support, test and 'pump prime' new projects. The rationale behind this fund should be argued for in the business plan as a sound management idea.

There is an emerging opinion amongst several observers that larger organisations find it much harder to do new things than smaller ones. In the private sector large conglomerates such as ICI and IBM have redesigned themselves into smaller units and encouraged decentralisation and task forces to get away from the notion that intelligent thinking and effective management are the province of the corporate headquarters. New ideas can get lost in office politics, demarcation battles and numerous committees and meetings.

> One senior manager in a large national charity described how he was trying to turn the organisation around:
>
> *'We are working hard to break down the barriers between our head office and local projects. We are reducing the number of things that need to come to us for approval, we are encouraging our project leaders to keep some time back for exploring local needs and planning new projects. We have created a small development budget to work on new ideas or to allow for staff cover to do project development work. We want to turn around the view that all ideas must come from the top. It has not been easy and will take a while to work properly.'*

Organisational structures and practices can easily, but unintentionally, discourage people from having or taking forward new ideas. Many organisations operate at, or even beyond, full capacity. Every hour is in demand and all income is tightly allocated to existing commitments. Most of our structures and practices are about controlling what is already happening rather than allowing space to develop new projects. Tight job descriptions mark off boundaries and can sometimes stop people seeing the whole picture. Narrowly written funding contracts and business plans mean that every ounce of resource is committed to existing projects and service delivery. The starting point for the budget process in most organisations is carrying on last year's commitments and they rarely create any space for new projects. A lack of any uncommitted money or working capital means that opportunities to develop new and worthwhile activities are missed.

Lost opportunities

There is an accounting term called 'opportunity cost'. It describes when an organisation is using all its existing resources or is so fully committed that it is unable to follow up or invest in a new opportunity that emerges.

An opportunity cost occurs when one decision or activity stops you from being able to do or follow up something else. For example, a contract with a local authority might be so demanding that it leaves you with no time to develop other projects, make contact with other purchasers or bid for other work. The opportunity cost of the local authority contract is the cost that you forego by not having the management time to develop other work and create other income.

Often we incur opportunity costs by being too busy and not having any uncommitted time or money to explore and test new ideas. The cost of being busy can be losing the opportunity to develop and innovate. Organisations can become inward looking. Opportunities are often ignored because we become so involved in what we are doing that we fail to keep in touch with new developments and ideas. It is important to commit time to finding out about new developments and spotting possible opportunities.

A director of a voluntary agency describes how he does this:

'I have a rule that I spend at least one day a month away from the agency, at conferences, visits to similar projects or with our main user groups. We are a well established and generally successful organisation. But I get concerned about being complacent and failing to develop. I push people to keep in touch with the outside world. It encourages us to question what we do and helps us to identify options and opportunities for development.'

Developing an idea into a proposal

The final stage in innovation is often the trickiest one. It involves persuading other people that there is a basis of a sound idea that should be considered further. The initial enthusiasm, creativeness and even excitement of the people who support the idea may clash with the caution of those who need to know that the idea is viable, feasible and relevant. The next chapter looks at different approaches to testing an idea's feasibility. There is a stage before that, which is to convince other people that the idea for a new project should be explored further.

It is easy to come up with reasons and objections as to why something will not work, why a new project is flawed and even why the people proposing it are naïve and not fully experienced. It is harder to achieve a balance between encouraging innovation and a realistic appraisal of the idea.

Start at the end innovation

One interesting technique in developing a vision for a new project is to start at the end and work backwards. This technique is commonly used in developing new technologies. The marketing departments of some computer companies have even been known to announce the intended launch of a new product before it has been fully designed. Innovators sketch out how you would like things to be, look and operate. Questions of how will it work, how much will it cost and how will it happen are suspended.

Once the end scenario is clear, work can begin on identifying how to overcome gaps between where we are now and where we want to be. It has three main advantages:

- It produces a very clear vision of what you want to achieve.
- It is future oriented. Its starting point is where you want to be rather than the problems and issues of the present.
- It gives a very clear goal by which to measure progress.

It also helps to make a distinction between 'ends' and 'means'. Ends are what you hope to achieve, make different or change. Means are the methods, activities and services you use to get there. For example, an advice service could make the following lists:

Ends	Means
People better informed about their rights	Accessible advice sessions
Combating poverty	Recruiting and training volunteer advice workers
Highlighting the need for effective measures to tackle poverty	Specialist legal services
	Social policy campaigning
	Telephone advice lines

We often spend too much time looking at the means to such an extent that the ends get lost or become vague. Sometimes we get involved in means that do not take us towards an end. In recent years the term 'outputs' has been used to describe the means and 'outcomes' to describe the ends.

Twenty-one statements designed to kill a new idea

It is easy to reject a new idea. Often organisations develop a style that encourages instant rejection or discourages new ideas. Some of the reasons may well be valid. Others may not:

1   Excellent idea ... let's set a committee to study it further
2   It needs considerable research
3   We are too busy with day to day work to go into it further
4   Why don't you write a detailed paper and come back in three months' time
5   There's no money in the budget for new ideas
6   They tried it at *xyz* agency and it didn't work
7   How do you know that it will still work in five years' time?
8   Interesting idea but let's talk about the details
9   If you produce a five year budget forecast and a five year cash flow projection, we will consider it further
10 Personally I think it is a good idea, but ... won't like it
11 Please ensure that everyone is consulted about it and happy with it before we discuss it further
12 Funders won't like it
13 It doesn't fit with our five year business plan
14 Let's remember to include it in our next five year plan
15 There could be risks involved
16 We will only move on it when every possible problem has been considered and worked through
17 We only do new projects when we have guaranteed permanent funding
18 This is just a passing fad ... I have seen it all before
19 Good idea, why don't you start on it straight away alongside all your other work?
20 We tried something similar five years ago and it didn't work
21 Isn't that a new idea?

Four factors are useful in the process of deciding to progress a new idea:

■   **Focus the discussion on the big picture**. The discussion should be on the need for the project, its possible benefits and how it could work. Factors such as detailed costings, who will fund it and who will staff it are probably unknown at this stage and should not dominate the discussion.

■   **Stress the vision**. Spend time on why the project is needed. Do not assume that people understand the context, specific situation and need for a new initiative. Often people presenting a new project have laboured on it for so long or are so enthusiastic about it that they fail to outline the need for it and the background.

■ **Acknowledge uncertainties and unknown details**. People introducing an idea at this stage can often disarm potential objections by drawing attention to things that need testing or further consideration. It is also useful to indicate possible risks rather than let people spot them and to look for agreement to consider it further rather than a complete agreement for immediate implementation.

■ **Actively seek allies**. A new project needs backing early on. A useful way of doing this is to listen to and acknowledge other people's ideas, reactions and suggestions. The project may fail if it seen as being an individual's pet project or hobby horse. Use people as sounding boards and ask them to add to your idea rather than find fault with it.

Innovation checklist

Does your organisation:

☐ Set aside time to look for new ideas?

☐ Have a budget to support innovation and the piloting of new ideas?

☐ Spot trends in user needs and in external developments?

☐ Encourage staff to develop ideas for new projects?

☐ Actively look for ideas for new projects as part of its forward planning process?

☐ Use techniques and processes to encourage creative thinking?

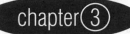

TESTING THE IDEA

This chapter looks at:

- When to skip a feasibility study
- How to test your idea
- What should be tested
- Feasibility studies
- Running a pilot project
- Deciding whether to go ahead with a project

Once you have decided you have an idea that is worth pursuing there are three ways forward:

- Carry out a feasibility study to check that there is a real need for the project and that the project will be able to make an impact on the need.
- Pilot the project on a smaller scale for a fixed time to see if it works.
- Skip the feasibility study and pilot project – just go ahead and do it.

The third choice may seem reckless and extreme. However, it is worth remembering that many effective projects and ideas would probably have failed a feasibility study.

When to skip a feasibility study

There are three main reasons for not carrying out a feasibility study:

- **Time is short.** Delaying the project while you do a feasibility study will only lose time. It is more important to do something than to wait.
- **You can live with it failing.** You have sufficient confidence and security to live with failure if it goes wrong and can cope with the risks involved in the project failing.
- **You can minimise risk.** The project is flexible enough to adapt to what works and stop what doesn't. It must be possible to change course or to close the project down painlessly if it clearly is not working.

How to test your idea

The way you test your idea will be determined by a number of factors:

- Potential funders' likely attitude.
- Your attitude to risk.
- Time and other available resources.

It is alleged that scientists at Farnborough carried out a laboratory research exercise into the aerodynamics of the bumblebee and concluded that it would never be able to fly. In many ways the only true test of whether a project will work is to try it out. Feasibility tests, pilot projects and market research are important, but cannot guarantee success or failure.

The factors for a successful project are varied. They include many human and one-off factors such as goodwill, luck and local circumstances. Many feasibility studies can be criticised for only dealing with objective information in an illogical world. There is a tendency to consider only hard facts and ignore information such as reactions, opinions and comments, which need more interpretation.

However, to overcome waste, convince funders and check out original plans, a project idea needs some kind of study to show that the idea is sound, could deliver results and is worth investing in.

Using a focus group

Testing an idea need not be a major task involving huge surveys and questionnaires. One common marketing technique is to run a focus group. Facilitators run a short discussion group with potential consumers and purchasers. The group only needs five or six members and meets only once or twice. The facilitator outlines the idea to be tested, works through a list of structured questions and encourages discussion.

One estate improvement project used this technique by running six separate focus groups for children, young people, single people, parents, older people and other agencies working on the estate. Two independent consultants acted as group leader and recorder. Each session started with a brief presentation of options for estate improvement.

The project director was very pleased with the results. 'We got much more useful information from the groups than we would have got from a survey. A lot of the most useful feedback was about people's preferences and informal opinions that a questionnaire cannot pick up. Many of the casual comments made about what would and would not work were the most useful ones. The groups were a conversation rather than a one way exercise. We intend to use different focus group throughout the project to monitor reaction.'

What should be tested

Six questions can form the basis of a new project's viability test:

- Is it really needed?
- Does it fit with other projects/activities?
- Will it attract sufficient resources?
- Does it have a body of support?
- Are the expected results realistic and worth the effort?
- Does it fit with what we want to do?

Is it really needed?

All projects should be aimed at meeting a need and making some kind of sustainable difference. But the history of voluntary and public sector projects includes several examples where a community's needs were ignored or a need was confusingly identified. Five things can go wrong.

Confusing needs and wants

Often discussion about what people need is passive, general and influenced strongly by what the people commissioning the study want to hear. This often happens when an established organisation decides to consult with its current or potential users. The discussion is usually constrained by existing services' and activities' boundaries. What a person wants is more about personal choice, aspirations and preferences. It might be ambitious to focus on wants rather than needs, but often it leads to a much more creative and effective project.

> A self-help agency consulted at length with the intended users of a new project. The results of the needs survey indicated that, of the suggested services, day care and counselling were those services most needed. Six months later the project was set up. Attendance at the day centre and take up of the counselling service were very poor. A casual conversation with two potential users indicated a likely reason. The needs survey was general and impersonal. They had answered the questions by thinking about what they thought 'average' users would want. They personally would not want to attend a day centre or counselling sessions, but at the time it seemed sensible to suggest that others would.

Only dealing with the surface problems

A useful approach to needs analysis is to recognise that a problem may have different layers, and that only some are immediately obvious. For example, problems of juvenile street crime will probably have a range of symptoms, problems and root causes. Lack of leisure facilities, youth unemployment, dysfunctional home life, inadequate policing, poor public safety and a lack of alternative role models are just some dimensions to a problem. It is easy to tackle only one or two dimensions (often those that you are most experienced or interested in) and ignore deeper or more complex aspects of a problem.

Often researchers are so interested in finding a solution that they do not spend sufficient time analysing the problem and challenging how it is presented.

Being fixed on the solution

Often a study is commissioned and carried out with a solution very clearly in mind. The problem is shaped to fit the solution.

> In one inner city area a respected community activist described what happens:
>
> *'We have had numerous vocational training programmes provided by central government. The courses have been good, but have not led to the economic regeneration that is needed. Indeed some local people are now on their third or fourth course. Training is important but it needs to go alongside job creation, small business support, child care, transport on and off the estate and basic educational skills. However, all the recent research work has only looked at training and not at the whole picture.'*

Not really listening

Occasionally there is a tokenistic or cynical approach to research and consultation. It is done in order to produce credibility and evidence to win funding. The overt or inherent assumption is that the research will find nothing that would challenge the assumptions behind the intended project. The project is already designed; all that is needed is some evidence that it is wanted.

Coping rather than changing

A useful test in designing a project is to think about the overall vision behind it. What kind of sustainable impact will it make? Will it really change things or will it merely make things more tolerable for a short time? Will the ideas behind the project make a real difference or will they only make a superficial change for a short period? What depth of intervention is needed? Is it better to do a few things that will create real change rather than spread resources widely and limit your impact?

Does it fit with other projects/activities?

A new project needs to be tested against existing or likely alternatives. Commercial organisations expect designers of new products to highlight their 'unique selling proposition' (USP) – what your project can do or deliver that others do not. A similar process needs to be adapted to test out the fit between a possible new project and its environment. There are two questions worth asking:

1 Who else is doing similar or related work?

A useful technique is to map out all other agencies and individuals doing similar or related work. It is important to think broadly. One or two comparisons will usually be obvious, but in time others may be identified.

2 Can the sector or market support a new project?

What is the size of the potential market? Is it cluttered with other projects competing for funds and clients? Is there clear space for a new project? What are the main trends in the sector or market? Is it likely that demand for the project will increase, stand still or decline?

It is also useful to compare the proposed project with existing or likely alternatives:

■ What will be different about your project?
■ What will it offer that will be distinctive?

Answers might point to what the project does and what it delivers or how it works or its relationships to its users. You need to be clear how you will measure the difference. Often the distinctive difference is more about how you do something rather than what you do.

■ Will its impact be greater or more distinctive?
■ What will your project do that others do not?
■ Will its impact be more relevant?
■ Will it be more effective?
■ Why will it work better?

If the project is unlikely to be much different or its impact is likely to be similar to or the same as existing projects, then the question of 'why bother?' must be raised. Why set up a new project if all it will do is duplicate existing work?

A project for changing things or making a marginal improvement?

In May 1994 two Indian community workers, Stan and Mari Thekaekara, spent a month in Britain looking at how poverty was being tackled in three areas. Their first impression was 'so many organisations and such a lot of resources, but why so little impact or change?'. They looked at how organisations identified needs and intervened, and recorded the following observation:

'The moment a problem is perceived, concerned individuals or organisations immediately concentrate their energies on trying to raise the necessary funds to tackle that particular problem. Translated, this means writing up a proposal then hunting round for somebody to fund it and finally setting up a project to deliver a service that addresses the particular problem of a particular group of people. And very often this service was of the highest order. But this does not lead to the eradication of poverty. It makes life more bearable for the concerned people. But the fear, the low esteem, the marginalisation – all remain.'

Will it attract sufficient resources?

At the start of any new project this question is often uppermost in people's thinking. Increasingly no certain answer is possible. Short-term funding programmes, changing priorities, political and economic uncertainty all make any long-term confidence about funding impossible. Conversely, this issue can be ignored by the promise or guarantee of initial funds for the first year or so (often with no guarantee of future funds).

Three questions are worth considering.

1 Does the project have a sound financial basis?

Detailed costing at this stage is difficult, but it should be possible to estimate the main costs involved in starting up and running the project. Are there particular aspects where costs are likely to be unusually high or difficult to control?

2 What assumptions can be made about likely income sources?

The accuracy of the information you collect here needs to be evaluated. You must balance optimism and realism. Some projects do not get off the ground because they are unable to prove beyond a shadow of a doubt that they will attract funding. Others are backed at this stage on the basis of vague promises of funding from unnamed backers. It is worthwhile collecting three types of information:

- **Indications of definite or highly probable income.** Funders may have indicated that they will back the project and provide funding or contracts. Unconditional promises are usually hard to find and difficult to get on paper.
- **Feedback from potential funders.** Informal soundings from potential backers can be very helpful. The idea of the project, but not the detail, should be market tested. Possible funders or purchasers should be approached to comment on how the project would fit with their priorities. Do they recognise the need? Could they ever envisage backing it?
- **Evidence of acceptability for statutory income.** Increasingly, projects operate in a regulatory environment in which, in order to operate and receive payment, clear standards have to be met. Examples include child care, residential care and legal aid services. Meeting these standards will have cost, time and staffing implications. Unless the standards can be met it is unlikely that the project will receive income.

You also need to consider the medium-term indications of funding. This may involve some realistic assessment of the stability of current income sources and the likely capacity to develop new ones.

3 What about non-financial resources?

Is the project dependent on volunteers, resources given in kind or other hidden income? How safe are these inputs? What would happen to the cost if they were withdrawn or declined?

One project was set up in a office donated by a local church and dependent on a team of volunteers. This support was taken for granted when the steering committee first discussed it. The appointment of a new vicar led to the project becoming homeless within its first few months. This led to the volunteers drifting away and no new volunteers being recruited. In a few months the project went from being promising to being a disaster. It had been set up 'on the cheap'. It had no contingency plans or thoughts about what could go wrong. It had assumed that goodwill would continue.

A sustainable proposal?

For six months a specialist advice agency had had informal discussions with the secretary of a charitable foundation about a possible new piece of work. The foundation indicated it was interested in funding a pilot project around the issue of small business debt. It wanted the agency to submit a proposal and wanted the project to demonstrate what could be done rather than simply a research need.

The foundation had made it very clear that it was only interested in funding a project for a maximum of 18 months. It wanted to stimulate new ideas and encourage mainstream funders to take up new work and would not consider funding ongoing commitments.

The grant would have paid for the wages of at least one and a half specialist workers and provided a management fee in recognition of the costs involved in running the project. Other obvious funders said that they were interested in the scheme, but did not hold out any real possibility of providing any new long-term funding.

When the possibility was discussed at a management committee there was a wide range of views expressed. Everyone recognised the need. It was noted that small business debt was a highly complex and drawn out area. Many cases could take years to resolve.

Three broad schools of thought emerged:

- Ignore the deadline. With luck something will turn up. All funding is good.
- Run it but be prepared to end it if necessary. Try to get other funders involved.
- Redesign and renegotiate it so that it can start and end within 18 months.

The discussion highlighted several critical issues in project design and development relating to risk, sustainability and the need for strategic thinking. The agency decided to proceed with the project only if the funder would agree that the project would be an action research into small business debt. The foundation rejected this and the project did not take place. The agency's manager commented:

'It was probably one of the hardest decisions we have ever made. To turn down funding runs contrary to the way that many voluntary organisations operate. But, from an organisational and service point of view it would have been irresponsible to have gone ahead with it.'

Does it have a body of support?

A simple test here is to map out what level of support there is within different groups, for example:

- direct users
- supporters
- decision makers
- people indirectly affected.

There needs to be a 'critical mass' of people who demonstrate a sense of ownership of and commitment to the project. They need to be prepared to invest their own time and effort and be willing to fight for it. This can be a difficult issue to assess.

A steering group set up to develop an environmental project was well attended and seemed to have the basis of a strong core group. It had met for nearly a year. The idea behind the group came from one person who had brought the steering group together. She did all the organising, drafted the plan and marketed the project. Very little was delegated to other members of the group. When she was ill for three weeks nothing happened. The planned steering group meeting went ahead, but was embarrassing. No one knew what was happening, no one even knew what needed discussing. What it revealed was that the vision and concept of the project was only held by one person. It was felt that to set up a project on that basis was flawed and would create a very vulnerable project. For the project to move forward the original innovator had to do less. Others had to be involved, not just as a supporting cast but as key players.

Are the expected results realistic and worth the effort?

You need to draw up a rough balance sheet to assess whether the work involved in setting up and running the project is likely to be paid back by the benefits generated. A traditional approach would be a value for money study. This involves testing the anticipated results against the criteria of:

Economy	Are the costs involved fair? Could it be done cheaper?
Efficiency	If it were organised better could we do more? Are the results worth the costs?
Effectiveness	Will it create real lasting benefit?

Such an approach depends on sufficient information being available. You also need to be able to make a fair comparison with other projects and have a clear sense of the value the project is trying to create.

An alternative and less financially driven approach is to predict what difference the project will realistically make in terms of what it creates and what it produces (the *outputs*) and what difference it will make for the users and society as a whole (the *outcomes*). Such predictions need to be carefully discussed and explored. The accuracy of any assumptions about what can be achieved and what can be sustained need to be evaluated.

It is important to test if the project will really make a difference. Often projects are set up without a sense of their possible impact.

> A project to introduce arts to isolated rural communities concentrated all its efforts on reaching as many people as possible. They felt that the issue of access was important to them and contact with high numbers would impress funders. The project's plan for the first two years would mean that people in each of the local communities would only get three or four two-hour sessions with the project. The actual value of this was questionable. Apart from a brief introduction to a new art form what real skills or insights could be developed? The benefits of the project were not obvious or sustainable.

Does it fit with what we want to do?

It is possible that an idea for a new project is sound, viable and sustainable but not the right one for an existing organisation to set up. Three issues are relevant:

- **Legal and constitutional fit.** The activities involved in a new project could take the organisation outside its remit. Its aims and objectives and area of benefit may stop the organisation from taking the project on. For example a charity's constitution may restrict it to operating in a particular geographic area or with a specific client group. It may decide that it does not wish to (or may not be able to) alter its governing documents to accommodate the project.

- **Synergy.** At some point an organisation's activities need to connect up. They need to create a whole picture. If they do not the organisation will become fragmented and lack purpose. New projects need to fit with existing activities. A director of a development agency commented 'Three years ago we went through a dreadful phase. We stopped being a united organisation and became a loose collection of projects that had little relationship to each other. Some were very practical, some experimental, others were about policy and research. We lost our identity.' You may need to discuss how broadly or how narrowly you seek synergy between projects may.

- **Skills and management fit.** It may be that an organisation does not have the right balance of skills to manage the project or may lack the structures to house it. If an existing organisation is not able to support or direct the project properly it will have a limited chance of success.

If the project is felt to be a good idea, but in the wrong organisation, you should consider options such as encouraging an independent project or transferring the idea to a more appropriate organisation.

Feasibility studies

Feasibility studies vary enormously in terms of scope, content and style. Some are the product of detailed independent research carried out to a strict methodology. Others are much more open-ended and deal more with people's opinions and impressions.

Types of studies

The six questions listed on page 31 provide a broad overview of the types of issues a feasibility study could explore, but in most cases it would be time consuming, expensive and unwieldy to examine all of them in detail. In broad terms there are three main types of study, and which type to use needs to be agreed at the outset.

Needs based

This type is focused much more on the need or problem identified than the proposed solution. It usually involves establishing exactly what problems exist, their size and extent and testing out how different solutions might overcome them. An example is assessing the causes of family break up in an area and from this research identifying the need for a family centre open at weekends.

Consultative

This is about 'testing the water' for a project. It is usually clear when the study is commissioned what sort of project is intended or is being actively considered. The aim of the study is to check that the project would be welcome, establish how best to organise and launch it and to see how it can best fit in with other agencies. For example, a steering group concerned with legal rights might carry out a feasibility study to determine how best a law centre could operate, what its priorities should be and how it should work alongside other advice agencies. The results of the plan will be used to shape their thinking as they develop their idea into a proposal.

Market based

This type of study is often commissioned when the project idea is at an advanced stage. Its objective is to test out with potential funders, users or customers the details of how it will operate. Its focus is on the detailed logistics and management. A new arts venue might commission such a study to assess anticipated audience levels, ticket prices and programme details. The findings of the study will play an important part in building up the centre's first business plan.

Designing a feasibility study

A useful approach is to design a project feasibility study around four key issues:

1 The idea and concept behind the project.
2 The project's feasibility.
3 The organisational, financial and business needs.
4 The factors needed for success.

1 The idea and concept behind the project

This section looks at the bigger picture. It tests the clarity of the original idea and challenges the assumptions underlying the project's idea. Typical questions include:

- What is different about this project?
- Is there a clear need for the project? Is the need fully understood?
- What are the alternatives to this project? What would be the short- to longer-term implications of not doing this project?
- What assumptions are inherent in the project's concept and design – do they stand up?

2 The project's feasibility

The main focus of this section is whether the project will deliver results that make the investment of resources worthwhile. Typical questions include:

- Is there any evidence that this sort of project has worked elsewhere?
- How might the project fit with and complement other services and initiatives?
- Are there any specific blocks or barriers that need to be addressed?
- Is there active support for this project from key players – e.g. funders and potential partners?

3 The organisational, financial and business needs

This section assesses what sort of structure, organisation and resources will be needed to deliver the project. Typical questions include:

- What sort of organisation is best needed to deliver the project?
- What level of staffing is needed to deliver the project?
- What sort of legal and organisational structure is needed?
- What sort of funding is needed – is such a level of funding viable?

4 The factors needed for success

This section looks at the levels of political, organisational and other forms of support the project will need to be a success. Typical questions include:

- How will we know if this project is a success?
- Who will have a stake in this project?
- Who needs actively to back this project?
- How can the project best be marketed?

Designing a feasibility study

There are three main areas that you can use to develop specific questions.

1 Which assumptions about our idea need testing?

Often the most fundamental assumptions are never checked or explicitly stated.

Assumptions to check include:

- Is there a real need for what we want to do?
- Is there really support for what we want to do?
- Do other people share our values and concerns?

2 What do we need to know to take this idea further?

It is useful to list the information and data you will need to consider the project further and work up a plan. Information needs could include:

- Current details of needs and local circumstances.
- Mapping other provision or similar activities.
- Available resources and their criteria.

3 What feedback do we need from other people about our idea?

Questions in this area relate more to people's reaction to the project. Possible issues include:

- Positive and negative reactions to the plan.
- Potential support, rivalry and opposition.
- Advice and ideas for the project.

Who should do it?

A feasibility study can be carried out by people already involved in the project, or people new to it, or a combination. People already involved may be able to draw up a study and carry it out. It will be important that they are able to think about and describe the project objectively and not see the study as a way of selling it.

There are people and institutions that undertake feasibility studies. Universities and colleges, consultancy practices and freelance consultants will all offer some expertise. It is important to shop around and find out about particular strengths and past experience. In working with both internal and external people it is important to agree and record clear terms of reference for the study at this stage. They should list the areas you want studied, the specific questions that you need answering and the timetable for the exercise.

One organisation successfully used a combination of internal and external people to carry out a feasibility study on a planned new project. A small steering group of staff and committee members was set up to work alongside an experienced consultant. The consultant helped to clarify the areas to test and designed the methodology. Interviews and consultations were carried out by three placement students and volunteers. Their results were collated and analysed by the consultant. The steering group studied the findings and prepared a final report.

Gathering information

When developing a new project you need accurate, relevant information to:

- Check your understanding about needs and problems.
- Show evidence of the need for the project.

Gathering information can be a long and exhausting task. There are dangers in overusing some sources of information or not fully interpreting the findings. There is also a danger of overusing hard information (statistics and data) and ignoring soft information (opinions and reactions).

Information sources

The following are examples of some of the most common sources of information on needs and trends:

- *The Indices of Deprivation* (Office of the Deputy Prime Minister). Measures of deprivation for every ward and local authority area in England. The index measures relative levels of needs across English local authority areas and provides a useful summary of data for each local authority area drawn from the census and from employment, health and education sources.
- *Annual Abstract of Statistics*. Compiled from over 100 sources, this contains statistics on the United Kingdom's economy, industry, society and demography presented in easy to read tables and backed up with explanatory notes and definitions.
- *General Household Survey*. Based on a continuous survey carried out by the Office for National Statistics, which collects information on a range of topics from people living in private households in Great Britain. The General Household Survey annual report series provides valuable data on people, families, households, burglaries, health and disability, employment, pensions, education, sport and leisure activities and housing.

- *Population Trends* (Office of Population Censuses and Surveys). Quarterly journal of statistics on population, childbirth, marriage, divorce, migration, death, abortion and statistics summaries.
- *Regional Trends* (Central Statistical Office). Official statistics about the regions of the UK. Covers social, demographic and economic topics. Includes a wide range of data from employment statistics to infant mortality, house prices to agricultural investment.
- *Social Trends* (Central Statistical Office). An annual review of British life. Well presented sections on a range of topics, from employment to leisure, education to health and transport to housing.
- *Neighbourhood Statistics Service*. An internet-based neighbourhood statistics service being developed by the Office for National Statistics. Initially, it will provide a database drawn from existing sources with local ward based information. Over time new sources as well as advanced search and analysis tools will be added.

The Office for National Statistics has a very useful web site at:
www.statistics.gov.uk
The publications listed are available from the Stationery Office: www.tso.co.uk
or phone 0870 600 5522.

Other sources of secondary information include:
- *Local statutory authorities*. Local authorities, heath authorities and quasi statutory bodies such as Learning and Skills Councils usually have a research and information section which should be able to advise on local issues. Published documents such as community care plans, children service plans or health authorities' annual reports should contain relevant information.
- *Other organisations*. Other projects may have published or unpublished information such as reports, service plans, user profiles and needs analyses.

Primary and secondary research

Primary research is gathering new information and conducting new studies of an issue or need. You might choose to commission or carry out some primary research into an area that you believe to be unexplored or needs looking at with a different insight. True primary research is unique and should have an unexplored line of enquiry. Secondary research is carried out by collecting, reviewing and interpreting existing evidence, data and findings.

Primary research methods include:

- Questionnaires
- Postal surveys
- Telephone surveys
- Interviews
- Group discussions
- Case reviews

Before commissioning original research, be sure it really is original. There is no point in duplicating someone else's work. One way of finding out if the work has been done already is to contact information officers in relevant organisations or to ask an experienced librarian to check research directories.

If you do decide to commission original research, be certain you know what you want and why. Research is all too often commissioned because nobody knows what else to do with an idea or a project proposal. Be clear about your needs.

Research is not worth doing unless it's done well – and that can be costly, especially if it is original enquiry. In quantitative research, sample sizes often have to be high to get statistically valid results. Get advice from professional researchers before you start – it may cost, but you could save money in the long run.

Secondary research involves finding relevant sources of information which can be used to test out needs and ideas. There are many sources of published research. You need to give careful thought to their appropriateness to your project.

Using the information

It is very easy to distort or misuse information, either intentionally or unintentionally. Changing the format of a graph can create a significantly different impression. Comparing one set of statistics with another may seem reasonable but may not be a relevant or fair fit.

You should keep the following points in mind when using statistical information:

- Often surveys cover such a wide area that they report on broad trends rather than specific needs.
- The time involved in designing a methodology, carrying out research, collating data and interpreting findings can be lengthy. Sometimes information arrives far too late for it to be useful.
- Often to make the research process and findings manageable information has to be aggregated. This makes real interpretation difficult. Research can raise as many questions as it answers.

Good information gathering should use a mixture of hard information gathered by primary and secondary research and allow space and time for gathering non-quantitative factors such as feedback, opinions and preferences.

Soft information is information that is usually not possible to reduce down to numbers. This could include people's emotional reaction to your idea, their personal preferences or opinions and odd bits of history, past experience or prejudice.

The balance between hard and soft information is interesting. Nowadays no computer manufacturer would launch a new system without taking into account factors such as 'user friendliness' or appearance. Yet ten years ago many computer manufacturers concentrated on technical performance and capacity. The growth of the personal computer market was driven as much, if not more, by soft factors such as design and accessibility. Getting the balance between hard and soft issues is now critical in determining the success of a product in the market. The project might be cost effective, logical, well organised and well planned, but for it to work there needs to be a feeling of enthusiasm, goodwill and energy.

Effective studies use a methodology that can pick up hard and soft information and ensure that it can be presented usefully.

Using the study's findings

The study's findings must be fed back quickly. There is little point in delaying since the basis of the findings is likely to change. The document or report is only a part of the feasibility study. People who worked on the study should also be able to talk about their impressions and assessment of the information presented.

You need to talk the conclusions through to see how they change the original idea or outline of the project. There needs to be a degree of discipline and objectivity in how this is done. Quite often, when presented with findings that challenge the original idea, over-enthusiastic and passionate innovators respond by questioning the study's methodology or validity. They shoot the messenger.

A well-designed feasibility study can provide valuable background to the decision to proceed, but cannot guarantee success or make the decision for you.

Outline structure of a feasibility study report

Introduction
Brief details as to how the study was commissioned. Who carried it out and when.

Background
Why was the study carried out? Was it to identify needs, check that a project would work or to test the market?

Assumptions before the study
A summary of the main assumptions the people who commissioned the study wanted testing. Examples might include 'the belief that a particular need is not being met' or that 'no other organisation is doing anything similar' or that 'this project could be self financing'.

Issues tested
List the questions that needed answering specifically and concisely as possible so that you can see whether the study has met the original needs.

Methodology
When and how the study was carried out. The techniques used to gather information and the organisations and people contacted.

Findings
The findings should be presented with as little commentary as possible. Thought should be given on how statistical information can best be shown and how opinions and reactions can best be presented.

Observations
The study team should be able to outline their main observations and their interpretation of any findings. They should be able to comment on any issues that may not have been part of the original brief but came to light during the study. Such side issues are often very useful.

How can the study inform the development of the plan
The findings need to be matched against any existing or proposed plan. In this section attention needs to be given to how the lessons from the study can be applied to any future project.

Main conclusions and recommendations
The main conclusions should summarise the study and draw from it any specific recommendations for future action.

Running a pilot project

A pilot project is a scaled down version of the intended project, aiming to do one or all of the following:

■ Field test the project to see if it works in practice.

■ Run it to see what successful features can be passed onto other projects and identify weaknesses that need solving before moving onto a larger scale.

■ To interest potential backers and supporters by showing a scaled down project in action. This is sometimes called a 'demonstration project'.

A project can be scaled down in several ways. It can operate in a narrower geographic area, work with fewer people or limit itself in scope or remit. Pilot projects need to be well designed. Thought needs to be given about how long a pilot has to run in order to draw conclusions. It is difficult to design the pilot so that it will be an accurate study in micro of the real thing.

The following points should be built into the design of any pilot:

■ **Make sure that the pilot can fail as well as succeed.** Often we learn more from things going wrong or not working out as intended. Pilot projects need to be encouraged to be experimental and be seen as a learning process. The reality is often different. Often the pressure is on to get it right first time and be totally successful. Staff employed on a pilot often pick up the message that if it works it will become permanent and will provide them with secure work. There is sometimes a belief that funders need to see a perfect working pilot before they commit themselves. These factors can hide learning, discourage experimentation and distort reality.

■ **Make sure that the pilot is as real as possible.** One national agency set up a pilot to demonstrate a strategy to involve young people in their communities. The 18-month pilot was a major success. It worked well, obtained a high profile, enthused people and prompted four neighbouring local authorities to agree to fund a project in their area. The four local projects did not work out as anticipated. Results were low. Huge amounts of time had to be spent fundraising and gaining access to key people rather than doing the work. One project was closed early. One probable reason for this was that the pilot received such a high profile and interest that was impossible to replicate into the mainstream projects. The attention of external evaluators, visitors from other authorities and media interest all encouraged people to make it work. For the pilot, doors were opened, money found and resources provided. The four mainstream projects were unable to command this degree of attention.

- **Build in review points.** It is important that learning and evaluation points are built into pilots. A variety of techniques such as diaries, review meetings, users, panels, external evaluations and interviews can be used to identify progress. They can help us to find out what works and why and, most importantly, help any projects that may follow to learn from the pilot's experience.

Deciding whether to go ahead with a project

Many projects just happen. No one ever really gives approval for them to go ahead. People just start them off and only talk to others about them when they need to (usually to get money). This is not a totally disastrous state of affairs. It can produce creative and imaginative projects. But it can also produce chaos and disorganisation. At worst, projects that fail can threaten the credibility or viability of the rest of the organisation.

A 'do nothing' alternative

A useful tool in making a case for a project is to indicate that you have actively considered the 'do nothing' alternative i.e. what would (or would not) happen if the project did not take place. This process is increasingly used by government in appraising regeneration projects.

A do nothing alternative analysis would include:

- What would be the short-term impact of the project not going ahead?
- What opportunities might be lost?
- Is there an argument that things might happen anyway regardless of the project?
- What might be the longer-term cost (to the community and also to the funder) of the project not happening?

The decision-making process needs to be carefully thought through. The right people will need to be involved. People with organisational responsibility (trustees, directors and managers) and people with a significant stake in it (staff, users and possibly funders) may need to be involved. They will need the right level of background information. They will all need to operate to the same criteria. Those involved in the early development of the project will need to be able to enthuse people to back it and at the same time be realistic about potential problems or unknown elements.

The board that would never say yes...

At her leaving party the co-ordinator of a regeneration agency described how trying to get her Board to back a new project was hard, exhausting and deeply frustrating.

'When presented with an idea for a project their immediate response was to ask for detailed information. This was often followed by a request for a feasibility study or a written business case or a detailed risk analysis. I would go off and do whatever was requested. Once presented with this information, they would then suggest a pilot project to see if it would work. Constant requests for new information and more evidence were a good way of avoiding making a definite decision.

'In the end I gave up progressing new ideas! By the time the Board gave it the green light, someone else had already started doing it and any enthusiasm for it had been lost!

'The Board often asked for relevant information and were diligent in their responsibility for managing risk – but they need to recognise that they have a role to create an atmosphere that encourages new ideas and innovation rather than grinds people down.'

There are several techniques to help this process, which is sometimes called 'project appraisal'.

Using a cost benefit study

A cost benefit study looks at all the potential costs and anticipated benefits from a project. It should look at all costs and benefits – not just financial – and also at short and longer term factors. It is a useful tool for summarising complex information and helping people reach a decision.

Analysis of the study can be built on by adding a points weighting to each factor:

- 3 points for very significant factors
- 2 points for significant factors
- 1 point for other factors

This is useful in determining how people see the importance of each factor and in giving an overall sense of the total cost and benefit of a project.

An example study

A national agency carried out a cost benefit study of creating a publishing unit to produce a limited number of publications and books. The study summarised all known costs and likely benefits.

Costs	Benefits
Start up costs of £10,000	Our membership provides an instant base market for most publications.
Break even point will be in year 2 or year 3 – we would have to underwrite this venture for at least two years	We have a unique position in the market. No other publisher has our expertise or connections
Price of each publication will have to be at least £10 to cover cost	Publications are an effective way of informing and disseminating our work – this would support our agreed strategic direction
Publishing is a volatile business. Costs and market trends can change quickly	In three years' time we anticipate this venture being self-financing and possibly creating a small income source
Will need a part time staff post in year 1	Publications will raise our profile. They will create broader interest, enhance public interest and media coverage

Risks analysis

All activity involves risk. The following risks are common in many projects:

- **Financial:** Costs could escalate or income not materialise.
- **Legal:** If the project does not work properly the organisation or individual trustees could face liabilities.
- **Credibility:** If the project fails the organisation's name and credibility could be damaged.
- **User:** If the project does not perform properly it could set back, harm or damage users.
- **Delivery:** The output of the project is not certain or within our control. We depend on other people or factors.

The project can then be evaluated under each of these risks. Likely risks are evaluated and action taken to minimise the risk.

A risk analysis matrix

The following matrix is a simple way of judging the risks involved in a project. It looks at the level of anticipated risks and compares it against the anticipated results.

There are four steps in using the exercise:

1   Decide on the project you want to test.
2   Ask if it faces high risks or low risks.
3   Ask if the results are likely to be low, medium or high.
4   Use this information to allocate your project to one of the four boxes.

Anticipated risks	Anticipated results	
	Low/medium results	*Medium/high results*
High risks	Box 1 Are the results worth the risks?	Box 2 How can we protect ourselves against the risks?
Low risks	Box 3 Is it worth doing?	Box 4 Do it!

Possible risks   **Possible results**
Financial risks   Volume of services and activity
Legal risks   Impact and outcomes
Credibility risks   Financial returns
Risks to the user

■   **Box 1 projects** (high risk and low/medium results) should be reviewed to see if they are really worth bothering with. The level of risk outweighs the anticipated results.

■   **Box 2 projects** (high risk and medium/high results) may be attractive given some kind of safety net or contingency plan. Can the risk be reduced, shared, protected against or insured?

■   **Box 3 projects** (low risk and low/medium results) may lack any sense of challenge or innovation. Are they worth the effort?

■   **Box 4 projects** (low risk and medium/high results), providing the assessments of anticipated returns and results are accurate, look worth backing.

Attitudes to risk

We need to look at our attitude to risk. There are two extreme positions: an unrestrained and reckless attitude that ignores risks in the pursuit of the goal, or a punctilious and cautious attitude that will only feel safe with a project in which every possible risk has been reduced. Both approaches are ineffective.

One strategy is to use a 'waterline' technique. New projects can be developed as we think best provided they do not endanger the parent organisation. The 'waterline' is the integrity, core values, financial balances and profile of the organisation.

Worst case scenario

A worst case scenario is an exercise in which pictures are drawn of the worst things that could happen to the project and their effect and implications. Possible scenarios include funding ceasing, key people leaving, drastic increase in competition and other such crises. Worst case scenarios are a useful way of assessing risks and identifying what safety nets are needed to protect the project.

Testing the idea checklist

Has your organisation:

☐ Decided if a feasibility study is needed?

☐ Got a clear idea of what is needed?

☐ Researched the market for the project?

☐ Identified alternatives to the project?

☐ Gauged the reaction of key stakeholders (e.g. potential users and funders) to the idea behind the project?

☐ Developed plans to avoid and manage key risks?

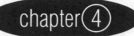

chapter 4

BUILDING THE CASE

This chapter looks at:

- Creating a steering group
- Producing a project outline
- Drawing up success criteria
- Building a network of support
- Developing a financing strategy

The main objective in this stage is to build up sufficient support from people and organisations whose involvement will be critical. The time involved can vary from a matter of weeks to a year or more. It needs to be carefully monitored with progress evaluated and tasks reviewed.

Creating a steering group

A small group of committed people is probably of more use than a larger group with differing levels of interest in and commitment to the idea behind the project. The group needs to be able to have the time to devote to setting up, running and building support for the project. This group may go on to become the project's first management committee, trustees or board.

A good steering group needs the right balance of relevant knowledge, contacts, expertise in funding and organisational management. All members need to have commitment to the project's vision and values. It may be possible to have people seconded to the group to develop the project or to use a consultant to aid the process.

The group needs to be task orientated, concerned about progress and able to build up enthusiasm for the project. It should not be seen as yet another committee or meeting to attend. Setting a time limit to the steering group stage often works well. If the group cannot get the project moving in, say, nine months then the whole idea may need to be reconsidered.

Producing a project outline

A project outline can have three main uses:

- The discipline of writing it can help the people who are promoting it to clarify their ideas and ensure that they have a unity of purpose.
- It can help to involve others. Targeted circulation of the outline to potential partners, backers and decision makers asking for their comments and interest can be an effective way of building up a network of support.
- It can encourage people to contribute to the detailed design stage. Their comments on the outline may be valuable in designing the project. Often the more people are involved in the early stages the greater the chance that they will be supportive later.

A good project outline needs to convey the following.

The project's overall vision and values

The project outline needs to set out in simple terms the 'big picture' for the project. It needs to communicate what the project hopes to achieve, why it is important and the benefits that can be expected. It should also highlight the core values or philosophy that underpins the project.

Evidence of needs

The need for the project should be set out by summarising relevant facts and evidence. This should be kept brief, but should be localised as much as possible. It may also be useful to link the needs into any statutory responsibilities or indicate how the project will work alongside other organisations.

Evidence that the project's ideas have been tested and could work

Evidence of past work, your track record, experience of running similar projects and results of any feasibility studies should be summarised to indicate that the project is realistic and has been tested. It might also be useful to indicate if the project is part of a wider organisation and, if so, how that organisation adds expertise, support and value to it.

The project's definition – a one page summary

This sheet captures all the key elements of the project's definition stage – as well as being a useful checklist it can also be an effective way of seeking approval for a project.

The project's background/context

Background

How did the idea for the project come about?
What are the issues and factors driving it?

How the project fits with our strategy

Show how the project fits in with our overall strategy and plan

The project's idea

The concept behind it
What's the 'big idea' and vision?

The need for it

Who will benefit

The deliverables

Outputs
What will the project do?

Outcomes
What will change as a result of the project?

Long-term gains
What will carry on after the project ends?

Resources

Resource need
What resource input is needed?

Funding strategy
How do we see the project being funded?

Other resources
What resources might we have to commit to the project?

How the project will work and what resources it will need

There should be a brief description of how you envisage the project working, its location, staffing and outline financial plans. This need only be a basic sketch of how you anticipate funding the project.

The document should be short. Two or three well designed pages should be sufficient to convey the main ideas. Its purpose is to stimulate interest and discussion. The style should be sharp, active and realistic. Make sure its objectives are achievable. It's worth keeping in mind the old marketing maxim, 'under commit and over deliver'.

> **Agreeing the project's brief**
> A project can be fast, cheap or good.
> You can have any two of the above.
> *Anon*

Drawing up success criteria

A very practical technique in developing a project is to draw up its success criteria. The technique centres on the question 'At the end of it, how will we know that the project has been a success?' It has three main benefits:

- It focuses the mind. People developing the project need to think clearly about its real impact. What will be sustainable?
- It can also help to agree a realistic vision for the project.
- It is a positive tool. Often in not for profit agencies words like 'success' are not used enough. The tool gives people working on the project something to aim at. It aids planning. Once the success criteria have been agreed planning can start by linking up where you want to get to with where you are now.

Different kinds of success

It is best to keep the success criteria brief. Writing them in headlines on one side of paper is much more useful than having lots of detailed criteria. It is very important to include a mixture of hard criteria (things that are easy to measure by counting) and soft criteria (things that usually require some kind of judgment).

Hard elements

- Keeping to target deadlines.
- Balancing the budget.
- The volume of output is in line with the project plan.
- The project is reliable and is well run.
- The project creates measurable added value.
- Activities and other projects will follow on from this project.

Soft elements

- Keeping stakeholders committed to the project throughout.
- The project causes minimal disruption.
- The output meets agreed quality measures.
- The project operates in line with our ethos and values.
- We learn from this project.
- The experience of the project is disseminated to others and influences their work.

An example of a project's success criteria

A small project set up to improve and develop the skills of voluntary management committees drew up the following success criteria for its two year project:

Hard criteria

- Between 400 and 600 trustees trained in their role and legal responsibilities.
- A core training programme, resource bank and other materials capable of being passed on to other network agencies in place by the end of the project.
- Two to four management support networks established, able to carry on meeting without external support.
- At least six local bodies' good practice consultancies carried out, and the main learning points of these studies disseminated.
- Funds and resources secured to ensure that trustee training will continue to be available in some form locally.
- A network in place of individuals and organisations able to demonstrate good practice and provide training and support to other groups.

Soft criteria

- A measurable improvement in the quality of governance and management within the local voluntary sector.
- Less conflict within agencies as a result of disagreements over roles and relationships.
- Increased awareness of the importance of good management practice and good governance in local agencies.
- The management of this project will be an example of good practice from which others can learn.

Building a network of support

A common tactical error is to see developing support and external contacts solely in terms of getting cash. Funding usually follows only after a relationship has been built, common interest established and confidence in the project's sponsors established. The objectives for this stage are to identify and make contact with people who may back the project now or in the future.

Identify stakeholders

A useful technique is to map all the people or organisations who are important to the project or have influence on its success.

They may include:

- Intended users and people connected to them.
- Sources of income.
- Supporters/volunteers.
- Decision makers.
- Regulators.
- Relevant communities.
- Potential partners and allies.

It is possible to map out your current relationship to them and their investment or interest in the project. From this it is useful to develop a strategy to market the project and develop a useful relationship.

It is worthwhile to look out for potential conflicts and tensions in the map. For example, a new project opening a hostel in a residential area may be able to predict some prejudice or anxiety from local neighbours. It needs to develop a strategy to manage this and create an effective relationship or at the very least minimise damage.

A community development project has used this technique on several occasions. Their development manager described how they work:

'As we develop a project in a new area we make up a list of all the people who are or should be significant to us. We spend time visiting them, explaining the project and asking for comments. We look at how we can overcome potential problems or correct misconceptions. I think that it is important to be open with people about our plans and be prepared to listen. Time spent building relationships early on always pays off.'

Mapping support

The steering group of a new project aimed to provide an alternative to custody for young offenders. Young people would work with the project to develop driving and vehicle maintenance skills as well as broader social education. The steering group drew up a map of existing and necessary relationships and placed the project at the centre. The position of each contact or interest represented the current state of the relationship. A short line between the project and contact represented a close relationship, a long line a distant one and a dotted line represented no contact or relationship.

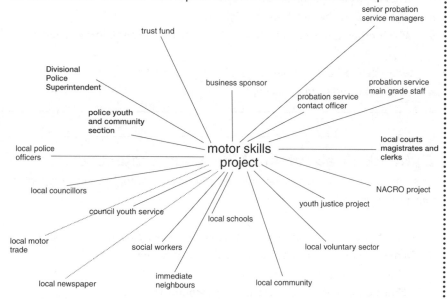

This mapping exercise highlighted three major issues:

1   The project had little direct contact with key policy makers such as senior probation service managers and local councillors. It had a fairly good relationship with frontline workers, but not with decision makers. The steering group drew up a list of individuals to talk to about the project and hopefully to win their support.

2   There were several people, such as the immediate neighbours, the local newspaper and the local motor trade, who had the potential to take a hostile attitude. The project agreed to produce some positive publicity material explaining the idea behind its work and to run two open days.

3   There were several people who worked in similar fields who would be important to the project. Some would be crucial in making sure it received referrals, others could feel the project was stepping on their ground and competing for funds. The group agreed to establish a project advisory group of interested professionals to ensure that the project complemented existing provision.

Questions to ask a project's stakeholders

- What would need to have happened in two years' time for you to describe this project as a success?
- What is needed from this project?
- What are the key things that the project must deliver?
- What is wanted?
- What concerns do you have about this project?
- How would you want to be involved in this project?
- What is needed to make this project work?
- Who needs to be involved in this project?
- Which other projects, activities and initiatives must this project feed into?
- What should be the main targets for this project?
- How would you judge quality?

Eight ideas about pitching your project

At some stage the project idea must be sold to other people to get support and win resources and co-operation.

Here are eight types of arguments that can be used to sell your project:

1 What acknowledged problem does the project aim to solve?
2 What emerging or potential problem does the project aim to tackle?
3 What opportunity might the project respond to?
4 What key policy or strategic direction might the project support?
5 What support does the project have already?
6 What tangible gains will the project deliver?
7 What other gains might the project create?
8 What might the negative impact or risk be of not going ahead with this project?

Making the argument

1 *What acknowledged problem does the project aim to solve?*
   Can you show that your project could deliver solutions to a recognised problem? Will the project create lasting success?
2 *What emerging or potential problem does the project aim to tackle?*
   Are the project's outcomes likely to be of a preventative nature? Will the project be an early intervention in tackling a problem?

3   *What opportunity might the project respond to?*
Is the project aimed at an external opportunity such as a new central government funding source? How might the project open up opportunities?

4   *What key policy or strategic direction might the project support?*
Can the project align itself with a relevant policy direction from central or local government? For example a health promotion agency was able to show that its projects linked in with relevant sections of the government's NHS plan and that by backing the project the local primary care group would be ensuring the local delivery of the plan.

5   *What support does the project already have?*
It is useful to list any support the project has already received. An environmental improvement project was able to convince a reluctant local authority to become involved by showing that active support had already been given by key community groups, the local MP and the parish council.

6   *What tangible gains will the project deliver?*
Can you show that the project's deliverables (i.e. what it will produce or provide) represent good or best value? How do they compare with the alternatives?

7   *What other gains might the project create?*
As well as producing tangible deliverables, projects often create other gains or useful outcomes. For example, a community safety project delivered by a number of agencies working together might also produce gains of shared learning, improved understanding and more inter-agency co-operation and joint working.

8   *What might the negative impact or risk be of not going ahead with this project?*
Think about what might happen if the project does not get support and does not go ahead. What opportunities might be lost? What might the impact be on the intended users? Can you build up an argument that not going ahead now could mean a more serious long-term need or a greater future cost?

Identifying who has a stake in the project

Stakeholder	What is their stake?	Positive issues	Negative issues	How to involve/action needed
Charitable trust (main funder)	Funding of £180,000 over three years	Want to back successful projects – if we can show that our approach works they may support us further	Physically distant Lots of competition for extension funding	Need to encourage the trust's staff and trustees to visit the project and share in successes Would the trust help us to evaluate the project and identify possible future funding?
Regeneration programme	Funding of £60,000 over three years Represented on steering group	Want to show that the project has contributed to the regeneration of the area	Not sure if they fully understand the ethos behind the project	Can we do a presentation to them on our role and anticipated outcomes?

Stakeholder	What is their stake?	Positive issues	Negative issues	How to involve/action needed
Host agency	Provides office space, management and admin support Represented on steering group	Key initiator of the project	Concerns about what happens in three years' time – will they have to pick up the work? Does the management fee fully cover their costs?	Need to involve fully in long-term planning Need to demonstrate results and outcomes
Users	Will spend time at the project – should benefit from it	Will they really gain anything?	Concern that it's just another project – will they gain anything from it?	Can we involve users in the planning?
Local community	The project will be in their neighbourhood Ward councillor is represented on steering group	Some recognition that young people need this kind of project	Concern has been expressed about bringing young criminals into the area	Need to build bridges and show that we are a good neighbour – consider holding an open day and producing a newsletter

Stakeholder	What is their stake?	Positive issues	Negative issues	How to involve/action needed
Probation service	Will refer users to us Claim to be 'Keen to support projects like ours'	Probation service's own strategic plan recognises that there is a gap for this kind of project	Some probation staff concerned about 'another short-term project'	Need to do presentations to all probation staff on what we can offer and encourage appropriate referrals Talk to probation's senior management about our long-term plans and the prospect of future funding.
Further education college	Some users may go on to be students College has offered to run taster courses and create access routes	The college is keen to be involved so it can raise	Will the college have the resources and budget to deliver its promises?	Secure formal agreement from the college. Should the college be represented on the project steering group?
Project staff	Will be employed by the host agency to work on the project for the next three years	Staff very committed to the project	Concern about short-term funding causing uncertainty and lack of job security	Need to develop good personnel policies and strong commitment to training and development Staff must be involved in developing exit strategy

Developing a financing strategy

Questions about who will pay for the project often crop up far too early. They block creativity and innovation. They are dealt with before the project's idea has been properly thought through. The cloth is cut to fit the price. It is important that the project outline is worked out before issues of financing are addressed.

The next chapter will go on to look at the detail of costing a project. At this stage it is important to explore the different types of income available, to draw up an outline cost structure and to develop a strategy to ensure income.

Thinking strategically about funding

Hashmere Skills Centre appointed a new director. The Centre was well-established and managed four projects, all connected to economic and community development. In his first few weeks the director realised that the way the Centre raised money for projects was at best confused and at worst chaotic. Three particular problems were evident:

1   Projects were often under-costed.
2   Enormous effort went into chasing tiny amounts of money.
3   The Centre did not manage its relations with the people who funded its work.

He persuaded the management board to set up a team to review and develop a strategy for funding future projects. Three members of the board worked with him. They reviewed previous projects, looked at how projects had been costed and interviewed representatives from their main funding bodies. Their report and recommendations were sharp:

■   One of the Centre's main income sources was the local Learning and Skills Council (LSC). The LSC staff knew very little about what the Centre did; they rarely visited the Centre and only received formal monitoring information about the statistical performance of projects.

■   The relationship with several of the Centre's backers was confused and out of date. The Centre used terms such as 'fundraising' and 'grant aid contribution' and referred to them as 'funders'. The various bodies who supported the Centre's projects wanted a much more active relationship than simply 'putting up the money'. They wanted a partnership centred on developing joint initiatives, sharing ideas and know-how and learning from each other. One programme manager commented that the only correspondence he ever had from the Centre were requests for money.

■   The Centre's backers needed to know (and good management suggested that the Centre also ought to know) what exactly a project would cost. They were not interested in making a financial contribution to the Centre's overall running costs in the hope that it would trickle down into projects. They had to know that their budget was being used to sponsor projects relevant to their objectives, accepting that a 'reasonable amount' could be paid as a management fee to the Centre.

The management board recognised that this approach would require a different approach from the Centre. They would probably have to spend more time getting and keeping project backers. Over six months the Centre took four main initiatives:

1 It implemented a marketing plan whereby key individuals from current and potential backers were invited to the Centre and encouraged to see themselves as investors in its success.
2 Potential backers were consulted at the ideas stage of a project rather than simply being asked to fund it. Their advice was asked for and reactions welcomed.
3 It developed a newsletter for 'partners' that gave quarterly information on developments at the Centre, progress reports and success stories. It was circulated widely in partner agencies, not just to their named contact officers. Its objective was to raise the profile of the project.
4 The Centre has moved away from a traditional budget and adopted a cost centre framework where each project is a centre. All costs are allocated to or shared out amongst the cost centres. For the first time the full cost of running a project is known and the full cost of some fundraising was clear.

The Centre director can point to early results of this plan. 'We do have a much closer relationship with our sponsors. In some cases we have had to do all of the work and force our way in. We are now being invited to work with them in a much more collaborative way, which is leading to some new (and properly resourced) projects.'

Balancing different types of income

Getting money for your project takes up an increasing amount of time. Policies, criteria and practices change regularly. In many instances the term 'funding' is becoming out of date. It is being replaced by contracts and agreements. The relationship is changing from one of grant giver and grant receiver to one based on carrying out a defined piece of work in return for a fee. Often an investment or a partnership relationship is preferred to the historic one of benevolent funder and worthy supplicant.

Balancing income is also harder. Many sources are becoming increasingly targeted and are reluctant to fund what has traditionally been called 'core costs' such as administration and management. Some income may be restricted or earmarked so that it can only be spent in an agreed way.

There are five main sources of income:

Statutory sources

Traditionally central and local government have grant aided projects to provide support. This relationship is in a state of flux. Several local authorities and health authorities have moved into a contractual relationship with voluntary organisations. Central government programmes, particularly those funding regeneration, increasingly regard voluntary projects as being part of the network that delivers their programme rather than a 'good cause to fund'. Open-ended grants where the public authority agrees to fund a project without stipulating what strings will be attached are few and far between for new projects.

Trust and foundations

The vast range of charitable trusts and foundations and corporate funding schemes operate very differently. Some are quite secretive in their affairs and operate mainly through personal contact and recommendation. Others have clear criteria and processes for awarding grants.

National Lottery

The Lottery distribution boards are transforming the opportunities available to fund new projects.

Public fundraising

The different methods of raising money from known supporters and the general public are well-documented and continually expanding. Public fundraising in its various guises has become much more competitive and consequently expensive. Shifting trends in giving and changing public opinion make reliance on regular public fundraising an unlikely option for many projects.

Earned income

Provided voluntary organisations keep within their charitable objectives they have the capacity to earn income through selling services. This can take the form of charging for activities through rent income, fees, charges and trading. Projects which plan to rely heavily on earned income should first test the market, understand how it works and be able to make informed judgments about how they will operate within the market.

In estimating income three balancing acts may need to be performed:

Statutory versus voluntary

A difficult ethical issue is how to define what activities should be regarded as statutory functions that the central or local state should provide directly or under contract, and what activities should be met through voluntary or charitable purposes. To what extent, if at all, should a project use resources provided by supporters and charitable income to support, complement or enhance services which we might expect to be statutory? For many agencies this has been a tricky line to draw.

Short-term and long-term income

Few sources of income offer projects the safe prospect of long-term guaranteed funding upon which to build long-term sustainable activities. Short-term funding can be hazardous. Several projects have been delighted by the interest and backing they attract when they are new only to find that interest is not there even two years down the road. Often being 'new' is a convincing reason why projects attract income. A project needs to weigh up the risks involved in starting up without strong indications of long-term funding or it must design its organisation so it they can be scaled down or closed without harm.

Earmarked and non-restricted funds

Often projects are started as a result of money becoming available that can only be spent on a particular activity. Examples might include statutory sources that restrict expenditure by criteria of geography, client group or activity, or income from fundraising where the donor has granted it on the express understanding that it can only be spent on a particular activity. The relationship between restricted and non-restricted funds is a tricky one. Over reliance on restricted funds can mean that the project becomes distorted. It is rich only in some parts.

The coordinator of a health project described how restricted funds caused problems for his new project.

'Over 45 per cent of our income for the first two years came from a health authority contract for work with young people. This money was tightly monitored by the authority who insisted that it could only be *spent on work with young people. This caused two problems for us. First, the issues we worked on were not particular to young people, but we had to bend the way we described and monitored our work to fit the contract's restriction. Secondly, the health authority was reluctant to allow for more than 7 per cent of the fee to go on project management costs. This caused us major problems when costing for other activities. Other projects had to contribute much more towards admin costs. In effect they subsidised the management costs of our work with young people.'*

An outline cost structure

At this stage you need to work out in broad terms how much the project will cost. This need not be a detailed exercise, but you will need outline figures to discuss with potential backers. Detailed costing techniques are discussed later in this book, but it is important not to underestimate the outline cost of the project. Promises made here that the project will operate on a low cost are inclined to come back and haunt you later.

Fundraising

Fundraising is now an industry. Consultancies and professional fundraisers are keen to offer advice, information and expertise (for a fee). However, it is important that devising a funding strategy for the project is a mainstream consideration rather than something which is abdicated to a fundraiser.

The funding strategy needs to be informed by the project outline, the project business plan, its anticipated balance of income sources and its outline cost structure. Lots of organisations waste time in fundraising by not having any clear sense of strategy and become driven by being busy rather than being effective.

The following are the basis of an effective strategy:

Research and test

Do not judge your fundraising work by the volume of activity you undertake. Lots of fundraising effort is worthy but wasted. The level of work involved does not merit the return. It is important to spend time researching the possible income sources available, finding out about relevant criteria and practice and deciding how best to make an approach. One national project employed a consultant to develop its funding strategy by testing the project on six field visits to possible local authority purchasers. In arranging the visits the consultant made it clear that she wanted advice and guidance rather than cash. In return the agency received some very useful feedback and advice which it used in designing its approaches to authorities.

Design a project marketing strategy

The term 'marketing' often confuses people. It is often wrongly seen as being entirely about selling. Effective marketing is different. It is about four elements:

- **Understanding how the market for the project operates.** How are decisions about resources made? How do other players in the market operate? What is the economic position of the market? Is spending likely to go up or down?
- **Determining how the project can best fit in the market.** What will the project do differently? Where should it focus its resources?
- **Deciding how best to enter the market.** How can it best be launched? Who are the key opinion formers? What would persuade and influence them to work with you?
- **Deciding how best to stay in the market.** What do we need to do to keep and improve our position?

A market survey

A voluntary organisation decided to develop a home support project to work with clients in their own homes. The service would be paid for by individual unit contracts for each client from the local social services department (SSD). The organisation carried out the following market audit, by talking to key people and asking their advice on how the project could best be developed.

Information	Marketing issues
How does the market operate?	
Client assessed by social worker	We would have to be on approved list. We meet criteria
Social worker picks service provider from approved list and district office arranges contract Service monitored by SSD	We would need good contacts and profile with local SSD managers
SSD has 'rate for the job' of £7.25 per hour Some potential for user to purchase extras	We would need high volume contracts to break even

SSD reviews prices annually Some flexibility for isolated adults	We should prepare costed menus of extra services
SSD has reputation for slow and erratic payment	We need to build in contingency for cash flow
Some private companies claim to operate at £5 per hour SSD is under very tight budget constraints	We could offer SSD a slightly reduced unit price for the guarantee of block volume purchase

How can we best fit?

SSD has had problems with two private companies Anxiety about poor quality and poor training of staff	We must stress our quality assurance and training programmes
SSD has had difficulty getting services in the East Division	Launch pilot in the East Division

How best to enter the market?

Central contracts team manages approved list	Prepare approved list application
Assistant director willing to consider block purchase	Present business plan and quality assurance system to SSD
Twenty-eight local area managers control spend budgets	Mail, visit and develop personal contacts with local managers Ask to speak at team meetings Invite SSD to participate in our training sessions

How best to stay in the market?

SSD becoming interested in quality assurance	Explore cost and benefits of quality assurance system
User feedback very important to SSD	Develop client feedback system and satisfaction audit
SSD recognises that there are some specialist needs this service may not meet	Keep some time aside for developing innovative services

Build interest and relationships

All too often new projects use a cold calling approach. They ask direct for funding without building relationships. A key part of the marketing strategy should be how to inform interest and involve potential backers. This might include testing your ideas on potential backers, asking for help, involving them in consultation on the project's outline and listening carefully to how the project can best work with them.

Recognise lead times

In most instances the time involved in introducing the project, developing interest, processing a funding application and getting a decision is underestimated. In the public sector the budget setting process is practically an all-year round activity. A new project has to win support from officers, win political backing, identify where funds can be taken from, go through a several stage priority bidding process and then be approved in a formal process. Early involvement and an understanding of the stages involved makes good sense.

The long decision

In one fairly typical (and reasonably well managed) local authority a national charity submitted a proposal to run a small project costing the authority £18,000. There was strong support within the authority for the project – indeed the agency had been encouraged by a senior manager to put forward a bid.

The timetable from early discussions to project agreement was over 18 months. In outline here is the chain of events:

January. Meetings with senior manager and lead councillors from the relevant service committee to discuss the project. Councillors and assistant director visit a similar project and are very impressed. No chance of funding until next financial year as decisions on available funding have already been made.

Late February. Urgent activity. Possibility that the department may have underspent in one area this year. The chance that the project could be started on this underspend was explored but failed to materialise.

April. New financial year.

May. Council's annual general meeting appoints new committee chairs. Meeting with the departmental assistant director to see if the project could be included in a package of projects in central government's Single

Regeneration Budget (SRB). The possibility of funding the project from the National Lottery is raised and dismissed.

June. The project will not go into the SRB as it does not fit the current criteria. The departmental director briefs the new chair and vice chair about the departmental strategic plan. The project is identified as being medium to high priority. Over the summer months reports are circulated that the council is likely to have to make up to 5 per cent savings in all service areas.

September. The charity is invited to contribute to a short training session for relevant departmental staff on the experience of the project elsewhere. The response is good. A meeting with the assistant director is positive. The project will go forward as one of the department's main bids.

October. The council's cabinet of leading members reviews future plans and is prepared to back the plan, provided officers find a way of reallocating current spending.

November. The charity is asked to prepare and present a business plan to council officers. Detailed discussion about costings, service plans and how the project fits with the department's priorities and existing services.

January. Positive indications from assistant director that there may be some space in the budget following a reorganisation.

February. Charity makes short presentation to council sub committee. Spending proposal discussed by the controlling political group and at the policy and resources committee. Charity asked to produce a scaled down project as a contingency measure.

March. Council budget approved, including a slightly reduced budget for the project. Negotiations with officers on the service contract between the charity and the council.

Three points are worth noting about this process:

- The charity spent most of its time building a relationship from which funding for a project would develop. It did not see the issue as simply being about fundraising.
- The internal process within the authority was complex. Power was shared between several parties. The charity needed to find out how decisions were made and how influence could best be exercised. Time spent doing this was worthwhile. It needed to find a key player, in this case an assistant director who advised and guided it through the process.
- The process took time. On more than one occasion the charity thought that the project would not happen. It had continually to alter its own

timescales and be prepared to some extent to change the design of the
project to fit with the authority's interests. Managing this was
particularly hard as the charity was concerned it could lose the project's
distinctiveness.

Make links

Few backers are now prepared to give money away without anticipating some
kind of direct or indirect connection. The funding strategy needs to identify what
kinds of mutual interest or need the project can satisfy. Possible interests may
include advancing a policy or social interest, extending learning or making an
impact. Talk the same language as your backers.

Learning the language

A whole new set of terms has developed in recent years to describe the complete
process of funding and managing projects. Here are some of the main terms used:

- **Added value.** The term is used to show how initial investment is enhanced or
  added to by what the project does with it. For example, a government scheme
  may provide funds of £30,000 for a project managed by a local agency. The
  agency uses volunteers, local contacts and expertise to deliver the project.
  These factors 'add value' to the original £30,000. It is possible to suggest an
  equivalent cash value of the added value factors.
- **Additionality.** Similar to added value, but usually referring to adding extra
  income. Initial funding to a project may be regarded as pump priming that
  aims to bring in other resources.
- **Best value.** A public sector process whereby a statutory body must review the
  ways in which it organises, manages or funds a particular service to show that
  it is providing best value. The review process should involve consultation with
  users and the public, comparing the cost and the performance of the service
  or project with others and challenging the basis upon which it is provided.
- **Business case.** A business case is used to set out the economic, organisational
  and overall benefits involved in a new activity. It is usually written by the
  bidder and is really a scaled-down version of a feasibility study and a business
  plan.
- **Business plan.** A written plan setting out the background, goals, strategy,
  financial and resource details of the project for the immediate future. The
  business plan makes the case for the organisation by setting out its strategy,
  intended activities and management arrangements. A business plan can last
  anywhere between one and five years.

- **Criteria.** The published statement of priorities and requirements that bidders need to follow to be successful in gaining backing.
- **Core funding.** The general non-project costs involved in running an organisation. Typical core costs would include administration, management support and general overheads. It is usually harder to raise money for core costs than for capital costs.
- **Delivery plan.** A statement of targeted outputs and outcomes that a project should achieve.
- **End date.** The agreed set date upon which the project or a key phase should cease.
- **Evaluation.** Evaluation looks at either the project's process (how it works) or the project's programme (what it delivers) to see if it meets its original goals and objectives.
- **Exit strategy.** A plan of what will happen at the end of the project and how the project will close down.
- **Impact.** What difference the project is able to effect. Impact is often the link between the project's outputs and it's longer-term outcomes.
- **Inputs.** The resources (finance, equipment and other resources) directed into a project.
- **Joined-up government or thinking.** Ensuring that services work together and are organised in way that makes sense for the user.
- **Leverage.** The process by which the project brings in other money. Several government schemes require bids to describe how, if successful, they will lever in private sector money.
- **Match funding.** Several funders, including some of the National Lottery Distribution Boards require bidders to put together a package of funding. They would fund a project up to a certain amount provided other income is guaranteed from other sources.
- **Milestones.** Key events marking a clear stage in completing a main stage of the project. Often the term 'landmark' is used instead.
- **Outputs.** What the project produces and delivers. Outputs are usually physical or measurable items.
- **Outcomes.** The benefits and overall difference that the project makes.
- **Performance measurement.** Pre-set measures or indicators by which the outputs and outcomes of the project will be measured.
- **Project appraisal.** The process of evaluating a proposed project to see if it is worth investing in.
- **Quality assurance.** Evidence of clear minimum standards showing the minimum levels of service and practice that should always operate.
- **Risk analysis.** A process of identifying the possible risks involved in an activity, assessing their likelihood and identifying preventative action.
- **Succession plan.** Another name for exit strategies.

- **Sustainable benefits.** Evidence that the longer-term impact and effect of the project has been thought about. Once a sustainable project has ended, other things (services, activities and relationships) should still be able to carry on.
- **Synergy.** How projects work together, avoid duplication of effort and create partnerships.
- **Targets.** Precept outputs or outcomes that the project should aim to meet.
- **Value for money.** A study of a project to check that the inputs are planned on a sound economic base, that the outputs are efficiently managed and that the outcomes are worthwhile and effective in meeting the original purpose or need.
- **Vision statement.** A broad statement of the overall goals and values that underpin the project.

Maintain the relationship

Many commercial businesses make the mistake of pursuing new business rather than consolidating and maintaining their existing customer base. Obtaining new business is expensive and time consuming compared with keeping what you already have. A key part of a funding strategy is to establish how to maintain and consolidate existing relationships by involving , communicating and working with existing backers. They should be seen as long-term investors, not completed sales.

Building the case checklist

Has your project:

- ☐ Produced an outline summarising the project's vision, the need for it and how it will work?

- ☐ Produced written success criteria setting out what the project aims to achieve?

- ☐ Identified the key group and individuals who might have a stake in the project?

- ☐ Identified how the project might be resourced?

- ☐ Developed a plan for how to build support for the project?

- ☐ Researched how potential funders make decisions?

- ☐ Identified the key points to make about the project when bidding for it?

chapter 5

MANAGING THE PROJECT

This chapter looks at:

- A project's structure
- A project's life cycle
- Why projects go wrong
- Projects and partnerships

Managing a project is different from managing a permanent function or unit.

A project's structure

Projects have some special features:

- **They operate to a fixed timescale.** Usually the one thing that is certain at the start of a project is when it will end. Managing something with a fixed life can be hard. The project needs to be up and running quickly, it needs to make an impact and complete its work before hitting its deadline. However, the project's legacy needs to be considered and planned for. At best, how can its work be carried on once it has closed? At worst, how can the project avoid creating a situation where people have begun to depend on it and expect it to be there just as it ends?
- **They usually involve several people.** Projects have a variety of individual and organisational stakeholders. The people who fund it, manage it, work on it, benefit from it or are affected by it all need to be involved. Yet they also need to be aware of the limits of their role.
- **Their structures and organisation are temporary and need to be assembled quickly.** Projects need to have clear objectives, plans and measures, and sound organisational systems and processes. They also need flexibility, independence and the ability to respond to new demands and developments.

A model for projects

- The **project funder or sponsor** is the agency that provides the resources for the project. It may have an active sponsoring role – the project might be its idea, it might have written the brief and commissioned the delivery of the project. Or it may simply have a funding role – it chose to back a bid to run a project.

- The **host agency** is usually a permanent body that has taken the decision to manage the project. The project might be an integral part of the host agency's work or the host agency's role might be a more detached one of providing a base for the project.
- The **project leader** is the individual responsible for delivering the project. She or he might be recruited and employed just to work on the project – when the project ends the contract ends – or might be a worker in the host agency who is seconded to work on the project.
- There may be a **project team** made up of people who will work with the project leader to deliver the project.
- The **project network** is an interesting concept. In their work on projects management Briner, Geddes and Hastings use the concept of an 'invisible project team' to describe this role (Briner et al., 1996). These are the people with whom the project needs to work to be successful. The support, goodwill and commitment of the project network will be crucial to the project's long-term success.
- The **end users** are the individuals or groups who should benefit from the project. They might be identifiable individuals or communities. Often contact with the end user comes via the project network.

Planning who will do what – roles and relations

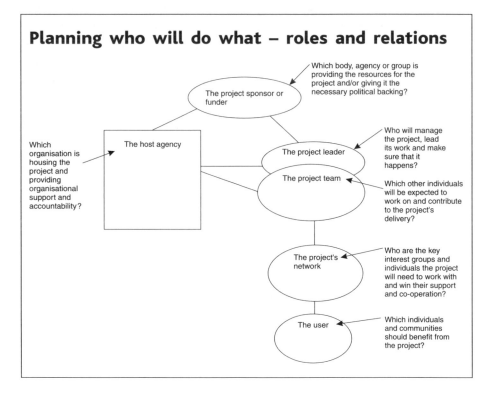

Getting it to work

There are four matters you need to consider.

Be clear how people should be involved

People are often keen to be involved at the start of a project. There is a high level of commitment. Sometimes this can lead to confusion about who is in charge and confused and conflicting reporting lines.

One of the key roles to get right is the involvement of the project's sponsor or funder. Some sponsors are happy to operate at distance from the project – they receive monitoring reports and send the cheque. Alternatively some, either directly or indirectly, want to become involved in the project's management processes.

> The project leader of a community health project described her relationship with her project's main funder:
>
> *'At one level their interest in the project was great. They wanted to attend meetings, were regularly coming up with new ideas and making suggestions as to how we should work and be organised. This was fine until their view clashed with the host agency's and our users' views of what was needed. I was stuck in the middle. I felt that I had two different bosses – both giving out different messages.'*

An over-involved project sponsor can cause confusion. An effective sponsor is focused on the impact that the project makes and the outcomes of its work rather than the detail of how it should be organised.

Clarify the role of the host agency

If a project is to be based in or sponsored by an established organisation it is important that the roles and relationship are clearly defined and recorded. A host agency can play three different roles:

■ **Being an incubator for a new project.** The host agency can provide an organisational greenhouse to help the project develop and become operational. This might be with a view to the project eventually becoming independent of the host agency.

- **Giving organisational and practical support.** The host agency can provide support such as staff supervision or help with planning and evaluation, as well as practical business services such as bookkeeping, payroll and an office base.
- **Providing links and connections for a project.** The project might be able to use the host agency's contacts, experience and local knowledge to help it become established. Being based in an agency with a successful track record of running in other projects might help the project to gain credibility and be effective.

The costs involved by the host agency incurred in running the project should be fully identified and included as a management charge in the project's budget.

Build the project's network early

The project's network can be made up of different people and interests:

- Representatives of key groups.
- People with whom the project needs to work.
- Key decision makers and opinion formers.
- People whose support and co-operation is needed.

The manager of a home care project described how he used this idea:

'We mapped out all the people who we needed to have on board –
social workers who would make referrals, social service managers and
politicians whose political and financial support we would need, self
help groups, user groups and staff in other voluntary agencies who we
would work with. We set about a process of contacting these people,
involving them in the project and ensuring that they knew what we
were doing. Early contact paid off. The relationships we built opened
doors for the project and in some cases created opportunities.'

The project network can play four key roles:

- A sounding board to test out ideas and plans.
- An 'early users' group to pilot and try out things.
- A consultative group to ensure that relevant interests know what the project is and will be doing.
- A legacy group for the project – when the project ends, members of the project network might be able to carry on its work.

The project leader's role is key

The project leader has a demanding role. She or he has the responsibility for making sure it all happens and that the project delivers. The leader must play several roles – strategist, marketer, fundraiser and manager – as well as carrying out the operational work. It is therefore important to make effective arrangements to ensure that the project leader is not just left to get on with it. At the very least the person will need systems for support, supervision and appraisal. She or he will also need to know what their delegated boundary is – how much independence is there to make decisions, set priorities and allocate resources?

When the project leader is working on the project alongside other duties it is important to agree how much time should be spent on the project.

A project's life cycle

A project has six stages:

- Defining and testing
- Gaining support
- Designing and planning
- Rolling it out
- Closing – the exit strategy
- Evaluation

Defining and testing

This stage is about having the idea for the project and defining and testing it. Often this stage is rushed – a project outline is pulled together to meet a funding bid deadline or the project outline is shaped purely to meet the perceived current interests of a particular funder. One project worker described how the first six months of a three year funded project were spent 'trying to find out what the person who wrote the funding application meant – what is described in the application bears no real relation to what is needed or wanted here!'

The definition stage consists of:

- Developing the 'big idea' for the project – what is the vision behind it?
- Turning the idea into a realistic project.
- Identifying what the project could deliver.
- Gathering evidence that the project is needed and could work.
- Testing the feasibility of the idea for the project.

Gaining support

In this stage the project needs to go from being an idea owned by one or two people to something backed and actively supported by others. It is important that the 'big idea' behind the project is communicated clearly. This stage is more than just getting funding for the project – it is about making people feel that they have contributed to the project's idea and design, and that it is relevant and has a critical mass of support.

Designing and planning

The design and planning stage is focused on shaping the project, making sure that it can be realistic, and the often difficult task of linking resources with priorities. Detailed work needs to be done on:

- The proposed organisational structure – whether it will be housed in a host organisation or be free-standing.
- The staffing structure.
- The budget.

Rolling it out

This is the implementation stage – the project is operational and is starting to deliver. It needs to monitor its activities. In this stage the project leader must ensure that people know what the project is doing and that early results are recorded and fed back.

Often the success of this stage is determined by the ability of the project leader to bring other people into the project and create team work and co-operation between different parties.

Closing – the exit strategy

This is often the hardest stage. The project needs to come to a smooth and orderly end, but a way must be found to carry on the work, ideas and energy developed. The needs of people working on the project and those who use it need managing. Experience suggests that the earlier an exit strategy can be developed and implemented then the greater the chance of a project ending well.

Evaluation

Project evaluation is about collecting evidence and feedback to show project funders and sponsors that the project has been worthwhile and also seeing what lessons can be learnt that can be carried into future activities and projects. Evaluation should not be an afterthought – it needs to be planned for at the start and the systems and measures used must be developed during the life of the project. It is also worthwhile to plan how the conclusions from the evaluation will be shared and disseminated.

Getting the stages in order

Often projects are so keen to be up and running that the definition and planning stages are missed or done too quickly. If this is the case the project may find it hard to identify, monitor and measure progress. Or in the absence of a clear brief and plan the project may take on too many activities and get pulled in too many directions. In this case the project leader may have to go back to the definition and planning stages. One of the hardest issues is making sure that the definition and planning stages have been done thoroughly and have involved key stakeholders.

Why projects go wrong

A group of experienced voluntary and public sector managers were asked to review projects in which they had been involved that had gone wrong. The projects had failed to deliver or were regarded as disappointing and had not lived up to their original hopes. The group identified ten common problems and some potential solutions.

1 The project is funder driven

Issue: The project exists mainly because a pot of money was found to fund it. All that is clear is its financial constraints.

Solution: The project needs to have a definition that takes into account user needs and expectations as well as resource issues.

2 The goal posts keep moving

Issue: There is pressure on the project to take on other things. There is a danger of the project drifting into new areas and losing sight of its original purpose.

Solution: Need to remind people about the project's purpose and either seek active support for it or go through a redefinition process. The project should not simply absorb new work.

3 The project has to beg, borrow and steal to operate

Issue: The project has not been costed properly. It takes up more time than was expected. The host agency has to subsidise it.

Solution: Need to cost the project properly and take into account the full cost of both the project's delivery and its management. The host agency should monitor its input and ensure that its resources do not leak into the project.

4   The project dabbles in too many areas

Issue: The project has taken on too much. It is trying to please too many people and will lose its identity.

Solution: Need to be clear in the definition stage about what the project will not do as well as what it will do.

5   The project loses its support

Issue: The project is no longer flavour of the month. Key players have lost interest and are drifting away.

Solution: The project should highlight what progress it has made and remind people of the original definition.

6   The project is bureaucratic

Issue: The project staff are spending too much time administering the project rather than doing the work.

Solution: Could some of this work be done by the host agency? A mid-point review might look at how the project is working and agree to change working practices.

7   The project ends badly

Issue: The project operated as if it were permanent. It ended in a rush when the funding ran out. Users had come to depend on it.

Solution: The project needs to have developed possible exit strategies to ensure that it ends smoothly and that the work is carried on in another format. The earlier that the work on the exit strategy can start the better.

8   No one knows what was achieved

Issue: Although the project was busy, no one can really identify what it achieved. A year or so after the project has closed people have forgotten all about it.

Solution: Regular milestone reviews and good performance measurement systems should highlight progress. A project evaluation should record the project's work and focus on what worked and learning points for future activities and projects.

9   The project lacks active supporters

Issue: The project depends totally on the project leader.

Solution: The project could develop a project team and also build a strong project network to include and involve more people. The project leader should become a facilitator and organiser of other people's involvement rather than the main deliverer of the project.

10   The project fails to communicate

Issue: No one knows what the project is doing. It springs things on people.

Solution: Communicating with stakeholders is a key role for the project leader. The leader must keep stakeholders involved and informed through regular contact and updates.

Projects and partnerships

A relatively new trend is encouragement from government to create partnerships between agencies and across sectors. Many new government initiatives for regeneration, health improvement and education have at their core the development of partnerships between public, private and voluntary sectors.

Partnerships can have different roles and scope:

■ Some are created to bid for money. Increasingly partnerships are assembled to bid to government for funding. The existence of the partnership demonstrates that all the main relevant interests are behind the bid.

■ Some are of a strategic nature. They commission projects, take an overview of needs and monitor progress.

■ Other partnerships are formed to deliver a project. They are practical and by bringing people together from different backgrounds and experience the project should be able to achieve more.

Partnership working can bring great benefits. It can draw in different skills and experience and start to break down some of the barriers that often stop effective delivery. However, often the good intentions behind partnership working fails to be carried forward.

A project manager for a health improvement project described her partnership project:

'It all started well, but soon problems emerged. All the professionals involved in the partnership – doctors, social workers, home visitors and teachers – spoke a different language and had a very different style of operating. After a few months it became obvious that several people were only involved in the project either to protect their patch or to grab money for their agency. When the programme ran into difficulties people started to drift away from the project and stopped turning up to meetings.'

Getting the partnership working

The following ten points can be helpful in getting a partnership working.

1   Clarify the formal arrangements

It is important for all parties to the partnership to understand what they are involved in. The following questions might help:

- Is there a lead body – does one of the partners have a special responsibility for convening and managing the partnership?
- Where does legal accountability lie? Who is responsible for employing staff and accountable for the budget?
- Where does management responsibility lie? Who directs the project and manages issues between partnership meetings?
- What powers does the partnership have? Is there a legal constitution? Are the groups that make up the partnership clear of any legal liability involved?

2   Work on a shared vision

Do not assume that everyone has the same view of the intended outcomes or end results. Time spent establishing a clear view of what you are coming together to achieve will help improve communication and build on a shared identity.

3   Identify what all partners can bring to it

A good way of making the partnership work is to identify what each partner brings to it. Some partners might bring resources and expertise. Others may bring less tangible things but are equally if not more important. For example, on a community safety project, the two representatives from the local residents association brought an understanding of the history, make up and culture of a local estate that none of the people from professional agencies had. Their 'know how' and local credibility was of considerable value.

4   Encourage joint training and sharing

Getting the people who make up the partnership working together and developing shared experience can speed up joint working, build good communication and break down traditional barriers.

5   Allow difference

It is important to recognise that a partnership-based project is built on differences. It isn't necessary for everyone to be and act the same, provided that they have signed up to the overall vision and strategy.

6   Be clear about delivery

Things 'don't just happen'. Just because a meeting has agreed that something will happen does not necessarily mean that it will. Systems need to be developed to ensure that responsibility for action is agreed and that progress is monitored and chased when lacking.

7   Ensure report backs

Make sure that people on the partnership are reporting back and involving their organisation and community. Producing simple progress notes and written project plans might encourage or remind people to report back.

8   Build in review sessions

Plan out simple review sessions. One interagency project has a six-monthly review session to discuss how the partnership is working, acknowledge progress and setbacks and check that the project's processes and ways of working are supporting involvement.

9   Monitor the levels of involvement

A useful exercise is occasionally to monitor the levels of involvement in the partnership. Who is participating? Who has fallen away? Is anyone having to take an unfair level of responsibility. It is also useful to identify if any key or new interests are missing from the partnership.

10   Plan for the partnership's future

As part of the review process it is worthwhile discussing the future of the partnership. Questions might include:

- Should it continue in its present form?
- How might it need to change?
- Will the current membership, structure and ways of working continue to meet our needs?

Managing projects checklist

Has your organisation:

- ☐ Agreed the roles to be played – by the sponsor, project leader, project team, host agency and project network?
- ☐ Agreed the role of and services to be provided by the host agency?
- ☐ Identified the people and groups it needs to influence and work with (the project network)?
- ☐ Ensured that adequate time is given to defining and planning the project?

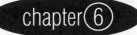

GETTING THE PROJECT GOING

This chapter looks at:

- Creating momentum for the project
- Agreeing the legal structure
- Developing a strategy
- Agreeing critical success factors
- Using milestones to identify progress

Creating momentum for the project

A new project needs to be able to move fast. It also needs to be able to involve other people, create alliances and support and make people feel that they have an investment in its success. The group at the centre of the project (and at this stage it needs to be a group rather than an individual) has to be able to juggle many different activities. They need to be able to make decisions on legal structures, organisational matters and financial issues, and at the same time create a feeling of energy and excitement around the project.

In this stage the people steering a new project need to be able to drive it and make sure that it progresses. They also need to create an effective style and process for the way that the project works. A project's perceived success is sometimes badly affected by how it relates to and involves people and agencies not directly involved. All too often people steering a new project work on it in isolation. They do not test or communicate their ideas. No one knows what they are doing. They spring surprises on people. Sometimes they are seen as being out of touch; even arrogant. The project idea may be imaginative and sound, but the way in which people learn about it, are introduced to it and become involved is crucial to the project's success.

In this phase three things must happen:

1 The project must take on an organised form.
2 The commitment and enthusiasm of the people around the project must be maintained.
3 The project must reach out to and involve other people.

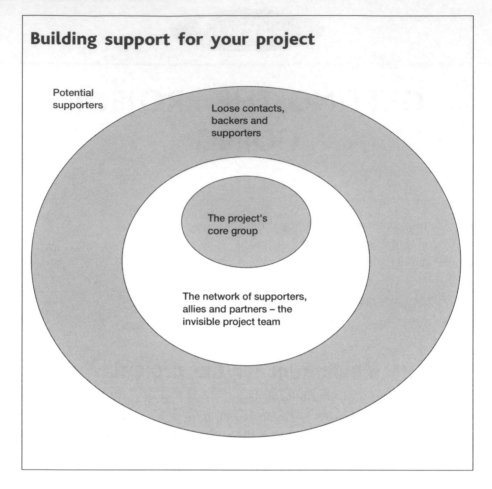

Building support for your project

Potential supporters

Loose contacts, backers and supporters

The project's core group

The network of supporters, allies and partners – the invisible project team

The project must make progress; it has deadlines to reach and work to be done. The people steering it need to become an effective team; they must be able to work together and make decisions quickly. However, for the project to work it must inform and involve other people.

The balance can easily be lost. Too much consultation and participation can delay decisions and stall progress. If the core team becomes too inward looking and adopts too strong an 'internal culture' it can put off others who need to be involved. Equally, the more people who are involved in a project, the harder it is to make decisions quickly and maintain a sense of ownership.

Projects at this stage have to build up momentum. They need to have organised the tasks necessary to get the project up and running. Responsibilities for making and carrying out decisions must be clearly understood. Progress needs to be monitored and early warning systems developed to ensure that if something is taking too long, remedial action can be taken.

Three things can be useful to help a project become task orientated:

Explicit rules about delegation, responsibility and accountability

Decision making is often painful in people-based organisations. A form of organisational 'ping pong' is played. An issue is bounced around from meeting to meeting, working group to individual until it runs out of steam or time. The issue becomes redundant. One health authority withdrew from contract negotiations to set up a community project with a voluntary organisation because it found it impossible to work with the project's representatives. Every decision and development had to be referred to a management committee that only met every few weeks. This dissipated the momentum behind the project.

Individuals should know exactly what they are responsible for, what decisions they can make and what they need to refer. Trust, good communication and accountability comes from clear rules rather than a vague commitment that 'we will all get on well together'.

There should be a clear plan of what needs to be done. There can be a vast range of activities involved in a project start-up. A useful process is to list them and allocate priorities. Getting the order right is important. A visible and active planning system can help this, provided it is regularly updated and monitored.

Methods for marking progress and achievements

Progress seems to create more progress. In this phase it is important to build up a feeling that you are making progress and are on course.

The steering group for an arts project started all its meetings by working through a progress checklist and highlighting action and events. It looked at what was stopping progress and agreed the next steps. Often the inevitable problems that occur in a project's start-up cast a shadow over any progress. This can demotivate and demoralise those involved.

Effective teamwork

Much of the literature and research on teams overlooks the point that teamwork is hard work. It sounds nice, but often is not. People confuse teamwork with getting on with people. Teams can degenerate into social meetings where several people meet and one or two people do all the work. However, for all its problems, teamwork is important in developing a project. It stops the project being too closely identified with one person, it brings in different skills and can strengthen the project.

A former director of a large agency described how his organisation often ran into problems.

'We stressed teamwork. As early as possible staff working on a project were encouraged to work together and see it as their project. During the development stages they were often almost invisible from the rest of the organisation as they worked away getting the project on line. The problem came when the project was introduced to others in the organisation. It was usually sprung on them. People often complained that they did not know anything about the project until it had started operating. They did not know how it affected their work. Recently we have improved how we set up projects. One particularly successful project was a campaign which during the development stage managed to create a strong campaign team and at the same time a visible network of people in the organisation whose commitment to it and goodwill would be critical to its eventual success.'

Effective teamwork does not just happen. The development of good teamwork needs to be encouraged. The following six points can help.

Good teams need a few clear rules

There is a paradox that the more flexible and informal your way of working, the more important it is to have firm rules that everyone keeps to, otherwise things can fall apart and become anarchic. Commonly agreed rules are needed about decision making power, communication, accountability and responsibilities.

Teams welcome and use diversity

Teamwork is not about all being the same. Often people join or are recruited to a project because they like, identify or fit with the other people. This is inevitable, but done to excess it can create an inward looking, 'clique' feel to the project. Good teams hold a common commitment to the project's vision and values, but are made up of people with different skills, backgrounds and experience. Good teamwork is not about everyone thinking and operating the same all of the time.

Teams need to know and exploit each member's skills

A useful team development tool is to ask each team member to complete a questionnaire auditing their skills, experience and contacts. This can be an enormous help to a new project. It can bring to light resources that were unknown and identify gaps the project will need to fill.

Teams need to be focused on making progress

During the start-up phase, the core group needs to be very task and goal orientated. They need to get the project up and running with firm and realistic targets.

The size of the team is important

Studies of effective teamwork suggest that a group of more than 12 people find it hard to operate as a team. It is difficult to communicate quickly, there is a lack of collective responsibility and accountability and it is harder to come to an agreement about how to work.

Teams use feedback, acknowledge progress and celebrate

Teams creating new projects need to keep themselves and the outside world informed of progress and achievements. One steering group of a new hostel produced a monthly 'project road map' as a way of identifying progress and problems and keeping their contacts informed. Progress should be acknowledged and celebrated as this creates the enthusiasm.

Agreeing the legal structure

As the project moves from being an idea to an organised form, important decisions need to be taken about what sort of legal structure is needed. It is best to make this sort of decision as early as possible. Creating a legal structure takes time and it is usually easier to set up a structure before the project has started operating rather than as an afterthought.

> ## Legal structures
>
> Two separate issues:
>
> *Issue 1*
>
> Should the organisation incorporate or should it remain an unincorporated body?
>
> *Issue 2*
>
> Are the objects of the organisation wholly charitable?

A critical decision is whether the project will be a separate, independent legal organisation, or become part of an existing organisation. Various factors need to be considered in making this choice.

Being a separate organisation may create a strong identity and help to form a clear vision and direction. However, time and resources will have to be allocated to setting up and running the organisation rather than doing the work of the project. In some cases the project may be so small or have such a short anticipated lifespan that it is not sensible to create a new organisation.

Operating as a project within an established organisation may help to keep costs down by sharing overheads and may make the project feel stronger. If the established organisation is effective, the project should be able to benefit from its contacts, expertise and management support. On the other hand, the project's identity and focus may be lost within a larger agency. Its reputation and direction could be constrained or even damaged by the parent body.

A possible half-way solution is to place the project in an established organisation during its first few years, with a clear agreement that after a certain time it will emerge as an independent body. Several organisations have started like this and several national and local development agencies such as councils for voluntary service have developed skills and experience in housing new projects.

The implications of being a project within an organisation

One of the most lively debates in organisational development in recent years has been the relationship within organisations between the centre and local units. Traditionally, organisations have been designed around command and control. The centre made most decisions, allocated and controlled resources and expected local units and projects to follow their line. In recent years things have changed, most notably in the private sector and some parts of the public sector. Much more has been delegated to local projects; they have been given independence and autonomy to act.

Areas for negotiation between a host agency and a project

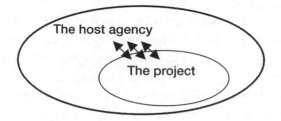

Tangible and practical services

■ The practical resources that will be allocated by the host agency to the project. These might include:
 − office space
 − equipment
 − use of the agency's staff time

Legal governance issues

■ A statement of who is the ultimate responsible body for the project. If the project is housed within an organisation then the governing body (i.e. trustees) are responsible. The project must work within the legal constraint set by the host agency's governing document.
■ Clear statement about who employs the project staff.
■ Clear statement about who owns the resources, equipment and material used by, allocated to or developed by the project.

Management issues

■ What is the management 'chain of command'?
■ Who is responsible for staff appointments, disciplinary and grievance issues, work planning and supervision?

Communication issues

■ How should the project keep the host agency involved and informed?
■ What sort of reports are needed?

Financial issues

■ What sort of financial contribution should the project make to the host agency to cover administrative overheads and management input?

Future intent

- How is the relationship intended to develop? Will the project always remain part of the host agency or might it float off and become a free standing and independent body?

In developing the agreement it is useful to work through a few questions:

- What would the process be for resolving a disagreement between the project and the host agency about future direction and work priorities?
  - How would changes in the project's forecasted income and expenditure be treated? What would happen if the project's income was less than anticipated or expenditure was greater than budgeted, or if the project started to generate income? Who would be responsible for financial accounting?
  - What would happen if the time spent on the project by the agency's staff was much greater than expected? How would this be monitored and resolved?
  - How would consistent poor performance by a project worker be monitored and resolved?

In deciding to create a project within an organisation issues of power, responsibility and delegation need to be agreed. Failure to do so can create major problems.

A group of teachers and educational psychologists developed a new way of working with difficult children. They were encouraged by a national charity to let the charity develop and manage their idea. A project was set up with staff employed by the charity and line managed by one of the charity's regional offices. The original group was involved in recruitment and was invited to form an advisory group to support the project. One of the original group members described the problems that started to emerge a few months after the project started operating:

'The project workers ended up being pulled between us and the regional office. There was a whole series of misunderstandings about good practice, values and direction. The managers from the regional office looked at things differently from us and at the end of the day they have the line management and financial power to direct the project. The advisory group is toothless.'

For a project to fit well within an organisation the following factors need attention.

Compatibility between the organisation's aims, objectives and values and the project's vision and values

The project must fit with the organisational, constitutional and managerial objectives. Its values and goals must be similar to those of the rest of the organisation. There needs to be a synergy of purpose. There also needs to be compatibility between the style, values and aspirations of the project and the sponsoring organisation.

Compatibility between the different projects run by the organisation

The project should complement other projects sponsored by the organisation.

> A large service delivery agency agreed to take on a project promoting user advocacy and rights. Some of the new project's work was perceived by other staff as being against them. It encouraged their users to make complaints and demand more rights. It created conflict between projects. The new project did not fit with the rest of the agency.

Clear agreement about delegation and policy

It is often assumed in organisations that rules and policies are clearly understood. You only find out that they exist when you step over them. Projects need to know their boundaries. They need to be clear about what is delegated to them, what decisions they can make and what issues need to be approved by the parent organisation.

Clear agreement about the management and use of resources

Increasingly organisations are cost or activity centring their budgets to show the full cost of operating a project. Done properly this can show the real cost of the project and the cost to the sponsor organisation of managing it, and encourage the project manager to exercise proper control.

Clear arrangements for employing and managing staff

Staff working in projects need to understand to whom and for what they are accountable.

> One national agency ran into several problems on this point. It encouraged local involvement in its community work projects and insisted that projects had local 'management committees' made up of local users and partners. The committees' terms of reference were never clear. Staff were employed by the national body and line managed by its staff. However, in two instances active local committee members operated as if staff were accountable to them. Confusion and conflict regularly ensued.

One useful idea is to set out the management relationship between a project and the sponsoring organisation. This can be particularly helpful if you want the project to operate at arm's length from the main organisation or if there is a strong possibility that the project could become fully independent at some stage. In the public sector this type of document (usually called a service level agreement) is common between service and support departments. It sets out measurable expectations in terms of service and standards.

Becoming a separate legal entity

Creating a project with a separate legal identity independent of any other organisation involves five main stages:

1   Decide whether the organisation is to become an incorporated body (usually a company limited by guarantee) or remain unincorporated.
2   Clarify whether the organisation's purposes are charitable.
3   Get advice and draft an appropriate governing document (constitution).
4   Decide who will be on the first governing body (management committee).
5   If appropriate, register as a company and/or charity.

Before starting these stages, one or two individuals must be appointed and have the time and access to external help to steer the process through.

This can be a time-consuming and complex business. It involves understanding different aspects of law and making sure people are fully aware of their individual and collective duties. It is useful to take advice at an early stage and discuss the different options, responsibilities and implications with an experienced adviser. Several national networks have produced model constitutions, which should speed the process. For example Community Matters produces a model constitution for community associations. The Charity Commission provides model documents for charitable companies, trusts and associations. Local councils for voluntary service or rural community councils should also be able to help.

Legal structures for projects with charitable objectives

The main legal distinction in structures is between being incorporated or unincorporated. An incorporated organisation has a legal identity independent of its members or trustees. It can enter into contracts and own property in its own right. An unincorporated body is recognised in law only as a group of individuals. As a body it has no separate legal status so, for example, property is held in the name of the trustees as individuals on behalf of the organisation. Any contracts are entered into by individuals acting on behalf of all members.

The main forms of unincorporated bodies are:

- An unincorporated association such as a club, society or similar association.
- A trust formed to pursue a purpose whereby individuals agree to act on trust to ensure that resources are used for the purposes prescribed. A trust is generally not a membership organisation.

The main forms of incorporated bodies used by charities are:

- A company limited by guarantee, where its members guarantee to provide a set amount (usually £1) if the company becomes insolvent.
- An industrial and provident society set up to trade as a bona fide co-operative or for the benefits of the community.

Charitable status

Registration as a charity is a separate issue from the question of incorporation. If an organisation's objectives are all wholly charitable as defined in law and it expects to have an annual income of £1000 or more it must register with the Charity Commission in England and Wales or apply to the Inland Revenue for recognition in Scotland or Northern Ireland.

Charities enjoy significant tax advantages and credibility in fundraising. However, having charitable objectives does place legal requirements on charitable trustees to ensure that the charity operates within charity law and limits particular types of political activities.

It is common for a voluntary organisation both to register as a charity and become a company limited by guarantee. Such a charity must then act within both charity and company law.

The governing body

All organisations have a governing body, often called the management committee or board. In charities the voting members of this body are charitable trustees. In charitable companies the committee members are also the directors. Members of the governing body have a responsibility to understand the law as it relates to their organisation and to have a broad awareness of contractual and other legal obligations such as leases and employment contracts. Failure to comply with the law could lead to civil and in some cases criminal action against individual members of the governing body. Failure to understand and monitor contracts could place the organisation in financial or other legal difficulties. If the organisation is unincorporated and cannot meet its debts, committee members could be made personally liable.

You need to take the following points into account when thinking about an organisation's legal structure:

Drafting the constitution

The constitution is a critical document for an independent project. It provides a framework for decision making, governance and management. Drafting it should not be seen as a legalistic chore. A useful way of studying a draft is to ask questions such as 'what if we wanted to merge with another organisation?' or 'how and when should the committee be elected?' The constitution should guide you through most everyday problems and situations.

Committee members' responsibilities

Many committee members only find out about their responsibilities by accident, and sometimes find out far too late. Committee members should receive information about and training in governance and legal and financial issues at the start of the project. This should be repeated for new members of the committee.

Liabilities can be personal

Failure to meet legal obligations under charity or company law can, in severe cases, carry criminal penalties and/or personal liabilities for debts. Responsibilities, obligations and their implications need to be discussed openly and honestly from the outset and the various types of insurance must be fully considered.

Sound management is vital

No legal structure can replace the need for accountability, effective communication and clear expectations between the governing body and the project's staff, users, volunteers and funders. Relying on trust and goodwill is not enough. It is easier and much more sensible to agree clear boundaries for making decisions, reporting lines and information flows at the start of a project rather than in response to a crisis. Members of the governing body have ultimate responsibility for the project. All decisions with significant or long-term financial or legal implications must be made by the governing body. They cannot be abdicated or delegated to staff.

Developing a strategy

During this stage an outline strategy for the project needs to take shape. Strategy is an overused word, used without clear definition or explanation. Many published strategies are far too vague and unrealistic. They avoid making difficult decisions about priorities and resources.

A good strategy has three elements:

- It links the project's overall vision and what it does in practice.
- It is about making priorities and should answer the question – how can we best use our resources to make the best impact?
- It sets out a clear direction for the project to follow.

The detail will be developed in the project's budget, business plan and work programme. At this stage it is important to agree a direction and statement of priorities for the project's first or first few years. It is important to think realistically. The strategy needs to be informed by answering the following questions:

- **How can we make the best impact with the resources available?** Mission and vision statements are not meant to give any sense of immediate direction. They are meant to provide an overall statement of purpose. Strategy should be concerned with impact and effectiveness. It should also link what you want to do and what you can do.
- **What can we do and what are other people best able to do?** Good strategy is informed by the outside world. In drawing up an outline strategy think carefully about how your project should fit with other agencies. How do you avoid duplication of effort? How can you create useful working relationships?
- **How do we keep the project distinctive?** It is usually important for a new project to have a strong identity. It will need to market and sell itself effectively. How will the project consolidate its unique selling proposition?

A project strategy checklist

Does it follow on from an agreed vision?
The strategy should be influenced by the vision that led to the project being set up. It should be guided by the vision, rather than by possible funding or by what you or your colleagues feel most confident about doing.

Is it based on an analysis of the world outside?
The strategy should be based on an informed understanding of what is happening in the project's environment. All too often strategies are drawn up with scant regard for the outside world. Planning needs to follow from and be informed by an honest analysis and appraisal of the project's environment.

Does it set out a definite direction for the project?
The strategy should enable you to carry out detailed planning. It should indicate both priorities and issues that might be important, but cannot be current priorities. Good strategies will indicate what you are *not* going to do as much as what you are. They are realistic.

Does it inform how you budget for and structure the project?
Questions of structure and resources should follow the agreement of a project's strategy, not dictate it. How you organise and how you intend to spend money should be determined by the strategy.

Is it clearly understood?
Can most people connected to the project summarise the strategy's key elements? Will individuals use the project's strategy to guide and inform the details of their work? Can you summarise it in three or four headlines?

Is it measurable?
Is the strategy written down in a clear enough way for you to be able to measure the project's performance and progress? Does it indicate key milestones? Does it help you establish a success criteria for the project?

■ **What should our priorities be?** The most difficult part of any discussion around strategy is agreeing what you are *not* going to do rather that agreeing what you are going to do. Once you have agreed your strategy there will probably be several activities and ideas that will have been dropped, discarded or postponed. Trying to do too many things kills many new projects. A few realistic priorities are much more useful than a vague wish list.

■ **What should the balance of our work be?** A new project should be able to identify different types of work. Some activities will be experimental and innovative. Others will be long-term and permanent. Some activities will be about service provision, others could be more about campaigning for change. A good strategy should create a manageable portfolio of work.

Formulating a project strategy
Be consistent about terminology

There is no clear definition about the hierarchy or exact meaning of terms such as aims, goals and objectives. Sometimes 'objectives' is used to describe the overarching purpose of a project. Others believe the term refers to the detailed and specific actions needed at any one time. Make sure that your use of such terms is defined and followed.

The plan should cascade down and follow a logical order. It is helpful to think of a plan as a having three levels:

1 Overall vision and purpose – the mission statement.
2 Main priorities and aims – the strategic direction.
3 Detailed objectives – the workplan for the project.

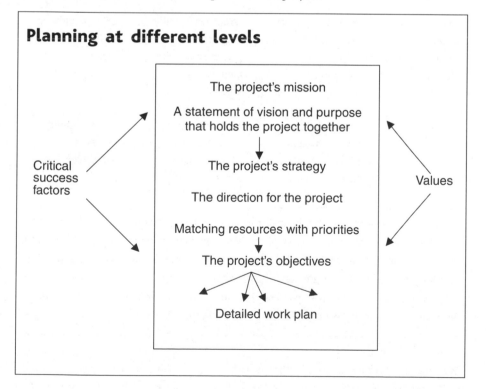

Planning at different levels

Critical success factors

The project's mission

A statement of vision and purpose that holds the project together

↓

The project's strategy

The direction for the project

Matching resources with priorities

↓

The project's objectives

Detailed work plan

Values

Element	What it is for	Example	Comment
Mission statement	To give an overarching statement of the project's purpose – its overall vision	'To overcome poverty by tackling long-term unemployment'	The statement should set out a clear vision that will last throughout the project
Strategy	The direction and priorities the project will follow to deliver its mission	'We will develop new services to support local community businesses'	The strategy sets out the project's direction and priorities in broad terms
Objectives	The details of the what the project will do and the resources involved	'By October we will have run ten business surgeries (with a maximum of 120 client spaces) at a cost of £5000'	The objectives are the project's workplan; they are the detail of how the strategy will be implemented
Critical success factors (CSFs)	Issues the project has to get right in order to be successful	'We must develop long-term partnerships with community groups'	CSFs provide an action list for the project's internal management
Values	Core beliefs, philosophy and ethos that are central to how the project works	'We will work with the most disadvantaged sections of the community'	Values should influence everything the project does

The mission statement should last throughout the project, it should not need constant reappraisal. Some parts of the strategy may also last, but priorities and direction will change periodically – they should be looked at least annually. The strategy should be sharp and set out an agreed direction. The objectives should be developed from the strategy. They should be task-orientated and measurable, and indicate who is responsible for their delivery.

The mission statement sets out the project's overall vision and purpose. It should briefly describe what the project is for and what it aims to do. The statement of strategic direction should give the project a clear guide about its main priorities at any one time. From this it should be possible to draw up workplans and action lists, and commit resources to a fixed timetable.

The mission statement should last throughout the project. Some parts of the strategy may last throughout the project, but priorities and direction will change periodically. The mission statement should not need constant reappraisal. The project's strategy should be looked at least annually. It should be sharp and set out an agreed direction. The objectives should be developed from the strategy, should be task orientated and measurable, and indicate who is responsible for delivering them.

Build in flexibility

Often project strategies are far too detailed – every pound is allocated and every hour is planned, possibly to impress or reassure funders. Certainly in the first year of the project it will be hard to programme everything. Retain some flexibility. The project needs a firm direction for its start-up and its first year. Effective project leadership is about operating flexibly within the overall plan.

Keep it measurable

Good measurement is important. It creates the feeling of making progress, it pinpoints problems and blocks and provides useful feedback and management information. The statement of direction and the detailed tactical issues need to be written in such a way that you are aware of what progress is being made and can identify achievements.

Assign responsibilities throughout

The strategy should indicate what is going to happen and who is responsible. It is easier to agree responsibilities before something goes wrong or does not happen than afterwards.

Focus on results

The language of the strategy must be practical, task orientated and precise. It should be about what will happen and what will be delivered rather than the detailed activities needed to get there. It should focus on the project's outputs and outcomes.

Agreeing critical success factors

A useful technique to focus a project is to identify its critical success factors – the key issues that need to be in place for the project to work. The process of agreeing critical success factors clarifies thinking, opens up communication amongst the project team and should help bring together effort and activity. It is best to have only a handful of critical success factors; too many and they will lose their significance.

Examples of critical success factors

External relations

- 'We need a high media profile.'
- 'We must build strong links with other bodies in our field.'
- 'We have to develop a positive relationship with our main backers.'

Internal relations

- 'A key factor is to sustain and develop a strong volunteer team.'
- 'We need to build the management skills of all unit leaders.'
- 'We must introduce a faster and reliable management information system.'

Style

- 'We have to encourage a culture that is innovative and allows risk.'
- 'We must keep the vision and values relevant and clear as the project expands.'
- 'We must find ways of listening to and learning from our users.'

Information and communication

- 'We have to find reliable formal communication between our three bases.'
- 'We have to be able to explain the project to new people in a succinct way.'
- 'We must improve the quality of our communication to the outside world.'

The critical success factors will change as the project develops. They set a leadership and management agenda for the project. Getting a project going involves a myriad of complex and demanding tasks and processes. It is easy to be sucked into being incredibly busy or to become obsessed with controlling and managing everything. The art of management is in knowing the main factors that need attention at any one time.

Using milestones to identify progress

In this stage it is worth identifying some key milestones to measure progress.

The steering group of a local children's charity identified five key milestones to achieve its goal of setting up a family centre:

■ Appointed trustees, applied for charity registration and started fundraising.

■ Appointed management group, consultants and freelance fundraiser.

■ Achieved income commitments up to £55,000.

■ Leased building and started to advertise for staff.

■ Agreed open date and planned launch.

The time between each milestone varied considerably. The chair of the trustees described their use: 'The milestones gave a discipline to our work. They provided a focus to our activity and stopped us galloping ahead. At each milestone the trustees reviewed progress and made sure that we were in a fit state to move onto the next set of tasks.'

Milestones work best if they are linked to the completion of key tasks. They are a landmark for the start-up phase. It is useful to agree an anticipated date when you expect a milestone to be achieved.

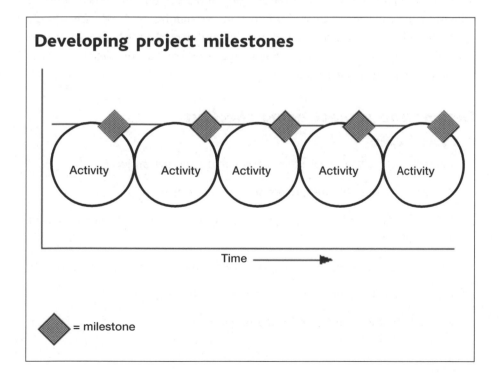

Developing project milestones

Activity   Activity   Activity   Activity   Activity

Time ⟶

◆ = milestone

On reaching a milestone the following should happen.

Progress is reviewed

Achieving the milestone shows that you are making progress. It is useful to spend time assessing the work done so far to establish what does and what does not work and to identify any learning points.

The project's original brief is validated

In reaching the milestone you may have learnt something that changes the original assumptions and thinking behind the project outline. Are the original plans still sound? Is the success criteria still attainable? What changes might be necessary in how you envisage the project working?

The detail for the next stage is agreed

The milestone review should be a useful opportunity to agree the who, what, when and how of the next stage of the project's start-up. Plans should be drawn up to take the project to the next milestone.

Progress is monitored and celebrated

Many of us have a problem acknowledging progress. But in some industries milestones are commonplace. For example, in the building trade when brickwork reaches roof height a milestone called 'topping out' is reached, which is sometimes marked with a celebration. This acknowledges work so far completed and gives people a feeling of making headway.

Getting the project going checklist

Has your project:

☐ Agreed what sort of legal structure is needed for the project?

☐ Agreed a strategy for the project setting out realistic priorities?

☐ Identified the people and groups the project needs to influence and work with (the project network)?

☐ Ensured that adequate time is given to defining and planning the project?

☐ Identified the key critical success factors for the project?

☐ Planned out the milestones for the project?

DESIGNING THE PROJECT

This chapter looks at:

- New thinking about work
- Developing the project's structure
- Costing the project
- Staffing the project
- Managing a fixed-term project

Often projects are not designed. They are thrown together to meet fast approaching deadlines. This chapter puts forward some practical ideas about how projects can be designed and outlines some new ways of organising work.

Four features make the design of projects important and different from how organisations have traditionally been established and managed:

- Projects need to be designed for organisational flexibility rather than permanence.
- Projects need structures and systems that enable them to move quickly rather than simply control resources.
- Projects need to be aware of the full costs of their activities.
- Most projects have a fixed term. There is a clear point in the future when the project will end.

New thinking about work

Most of today's organisations were designed to be permanent rather than carry out short-term or project-based work. They were intended to minimise change and allow for command and control from the top down. They worked fairly well provided little changed. They provided continuity, certainty and control. Key principles of the organisational design were:

- **A clear hierarchical structure.** Policy and strategy making was carried out at the top. Service delivery was at the bottom. Some thought and others acted. Often the number of levels or compartments in a structure grew rapidly. Very tight spans of control were created. The more contact you had with the user the fewer rewards you received. Resources such as finance were held centrally and tightly controlled.

Old and new organisational design ideas

Old idea	New idea
Built to last	Built to change
Designed to be permanent	Designed to be flexible
Need to cope with incremental change	Need to live with constant change
	Don't assume that anything will stay the same
Strict hierarchy of control	Networks
Command and control from the top down	Everything should be task oriented
Job descriptions highly defined	Flexible job roles
Status and position important	Emphasis on teams
Detailed plans and budgets	Strategic thinking
Strong belief in long-term paper planning	Must be able to spot and quickly respond to external trends
Tight control of all resources	Resources must be managed flexibly to meet changes
Central control	Much more delegation and devolution of power and resources
Uniform employment systems	Variety of employment arrangements
Standard employment rules and conditions for all contracts	Increased use of short-term freelance staff, associates and secondments as and when needed

- **Tight boundaries.** Most organisations used departmental, professional or geographic divides as the key organisational building blocks. You knew your job and you kept to it. This often created tension within the organisation as different groups clashed and played out office politics or work fell between two places.
- **Communication came from the top down.** Little formal communication went up or across the organisation.

Constant changes have found these design principles to be lacking. New needs emerge faster. Technology is changing how we can work. Changes in policy, funding and the external environment seem to happen much more frequently.

> 'So much of what we call management consists of making it difficult for people to work'
> *Peter F Drucker*

Narrow job design, strict boundaries and top heavy structures made change, teamwork and flexibility difficult. Traditional thinking about management also produced a fragmented organisation in which few people saw the whole picture: people only saw their bit of it.

Projects today

Projects need to be designed with the following four features in mind:

- **The project needs to be focused on results.** People and resources must be used flexibly within the project to meet its end. The project needs to be geared up to meet its tasks rather than simply exist within the structure.
- **Everyone in the project must see the big picture.** Projects usually have very flat structures so everyone can keep in touch and feel part of the project. Everyone involved must feel committed to the whole project, not just their part of it.
- **The project's structure must enable it to change as required.** Projects go through different phases. The kind of work needed in the start-up phase will be different from work needed in the main part of the project or at its end. Staff roles and responsibilities need to be adaptable. Many aspects of the project will be temporary rather than fixed.
- **Teamwork as a building block.** In smaller projects staff need to be flexible in how they operate and will often work without much direct supervision. Projects need to consider recruiting people who are experienced in teamwork, are able to cover for and support other team members and can possibly become multi-skilled.

Strategy versus structure

There are not many established rules on how to design an organisation. One of the few well established rules is that decisions need to be made about strategy (i.e. what you are going to do) before you agree how you are going to do it.

Often the structures and systems we have restrict and limit the strategy that we can follow. Badly designed job descriptions, staff structures and other systems can get in the way of the project.

> A director of a specialist advice agency described her experience of this issue:
>
> *'When we set up the project we made very quick decisions about what sort of jobs we would need. We recruited people for their particular technical competence. We started out with three individuals who were experts in their own fields. However, the project's plan requires them to take on pieces of work that require a broad range of skills. Often they have to work as trainers or local advisers and operate outside of their specialist boundary. The job roles that we agreed and recruited against have created a structure that works against our strategy.'*

Structural and system factors such as job roles, reporting relationships, budget and resource controls and even factors such as office layouts all have a major impact on how we work. They need, therefore, to be designed after you have agreed the project's overall strategic direction and priorities.

Developing the project's structure

Structures and systems need to fit the project, rather than the project having to fit in with existing structures and systems. Often when we design a new project we are inclined to copy how large and established organisations work.

> One new campaign group was set up by a group of activists who worked mainly in the public sector. Their project draft included a committee structure that reflected their experience of working in a large organisation. The staff team spent most of its first year struggling to service the organisational bureaucracy and controls. The new campaign director had to fight hard to persuade them to reduce the number of meetings and standing sub-committees from six to two, renegotiate staff job

descriptions to include flexibility as a main task and reduce the number of paper reports required.

The following points are useful in building a flexible project structure.

Make delegation of responsibilities and decision making explicit

Often lines of responsibility are never made clear. The boundary of what you can do, how much money you can spend or what decisions you can make only become clear once you overstep them. It is easier to agree and review boundaries in advance rather than after a problem. Good delegation should include tasks (i.e. what work you have to do) and what decisions you can make. Some organisations are very good at delegating (or even dumping) work, but not so good at delegating decision making power.

Keep the remit of committees focused

The remit and responsibilities of management boards or committees need to be agreed and documented. People must be clear about the decisions the committee has to make and what information the committee needs to make informed decisions.

Watch out for a 'democratic overload'

Even in quite small projects meetings can take over. Sub-committees and working groups are formed to work on an issue or even as a way of pretending to make progress. With the exception of the main management committee, the need for committees, sub groups and meetings should be looked at regularly. If they are not 'adding value' to the project and simply have become part of an organisational routine they should be cut down.

Budget for flexibility

Projects often need a budgeting system that allows for some flexibility. The project may have to move cash between budget headings to allow for changed patterns of needs. The project may need occasional access to funds to develop new work and follow up opportunities. Certainly in the first year or so the budget should be able to support reasonable flexibility.

Identify relevant performance measures

Measurement is important to monitor the project's work and ensure progress towards its milestones and overall goals. The management committee should agree some simple measures to ensure it is informed of progress. Be careful not to have too many. A few well chosen measures should act as a project's dashboard to help it steer and alert it to any problems.

Use information technology intelligently

Most organisations have computers. However, in offices, most computers are grossly underused. Often the use of technology is not planned and training and support is not budgeted for. Technology is only used to automate what was previously done by hand. The potential of electronic mail to aid communication, and databases and other systems to help with other tasks is often overlooked. Seeing technology as a vital part of the project's organisation and planning how best to use it from the outset can be time saving.

Control paperwork

Organisations often drown in paperwork. From the start encourage people to communicate in plain English. Avoid long reports and unnecessary systems and procedures.

Build in periodic organisational reviews

It is useful to review early on in a project how well the organisational systems and structures are helping to achieve the project's strategy. One health agency holds a two hour organisational 'fitness workshop' three times a year. Blocks and barriers to effective teamwork, communication and progress are identified and eliminated. Even in a small agency unnecessary systems and bureaucracy can creep up quickly.

Common project design faults

Often organisations create structures that do not work. Here are some common examples.

The one person project

When is a project too small to be an effective organisation?

> The sole employee of a self help agency described her role as 'project director, fundraiser, ideas person, administrator, editor, office cleaner, bookkeeper and anything else that is thrown at me'. She had so many roles and expectations placed on her that the job was impossible.

Everything depended on her. The management committee was committed but lacked the time to give support. Most of the employee's time was spent on keeping the organisation together rather than providing direct services. Often she was isolated, did not feel part of anything and lacked access to any support or supervision.

Rather than becoming a separate project the committee might have explored ways of housing the project within an existing organisation or contracting out some of the activities. Projects built around one key worker only work if considerable support, supervision and review mechanisms are built in.

The top heavy project

As part of a time management course the three workers of an education project recorded how they actually spent their time in quarter hour intervals. They were shocked to learn that nearly 60 per cent of their combined time went on servicing the organisation, attending meetings and preparing reports. The project had allowed a system of meetings, committees, reports and other aspects of internal bureaucracy to grow and multiply. It had an organisational structure that was far too large and time consuming in proportion to the size and work of the project.

Systems and structures are important, but do have a habit of propagating. Meetings take place because they are scheduled rather than needed, long reports look better than shorter ones and technology provides information that is rarely used, but looks interesting. It is worthwhile regularly checking the balance between time spent on direct or primary activities and on indirect or internal activities. It is also useful to prune administrative systems and processes periodically.

The open ended job

Job descriptions are usually written to make sure that every possible activity is included to prevent conflicts. Often new postholders have to spend the first few months of the project working out exactly what the job is for. Vague titles (such as 'development officer') and long lists of possible tasks give little clue about what is really important in the job and what kind of impact you need to make. All too often individuals do the part of the job that they like or understand best.

It is important to be clear exactly what is expected of a job. What difference can an individual make? What should their priorities be? How will you measure success? Well-written descriptions, efficient induction and probationary reviews for new workers, regular reviews and work planning can all help to overcome this problem.

The powerless assistant/deputy

Often as a project expands it simply adds to its structure, rather than thinking about it. A common method is to give the hard-pressed, senior person in the project a deputy or assistant as a way of helping them. This type of role can only work if certain tasks are clearly delegated and the deputy has some autonomy. All too often deputies and assistants become human 'dumping grounds' for things that their boss no longer wants to do. They lack any independent authority or power. They are understudies.

It is better to review how tasks and responsibilities can be reallocated amongst existing staff and, if needed, create a new post with clear responsibilities and tasks. Staff may still report to the senior person, but not as a stand in.

Issue = job

> One national agency has a track record that whenever it identifies a policy or controversial issue it creates a job (or if it is a big issue it creates a whole project). Over the past ten years it has set up an equal opportunities project, user involvement officer and, most recently, an environmental issues project. Setting up these projects creates an illusion that the agency is committed to and making progress on the issue. The reality is different. In all cases new postholders have to spend time trying to define exactly what is expected of them. In several cases, by the time they have been appointed the organisation has lost interest in the issue and moved on to other things.

Good projects and good jobs are task rather than 'policy issue' orientated. If you cannot measure performance or identify a criteria for success, or are confused about the desired outcomes then you need further thinking and discussion. Probably the worst thing to do would be to move straight to action and create a project.

Sealed containers in the organisation

> A local housing agency grew in traditional pattern. It created jobs, and then departments, based around the traditional job areas – housing

management, maintenance, finance, development and the director's office. Very quickly the five departments started to define how they wanted to organise their work. Over time it became obvious that tenants had to deal with several individuals to get a problem solved. In the old days one person could assess a problem and plan the solution and if they couldn't deal with it call in a contractor. Nowadays, issues are referred to different departments, all with their own systems and procedures. Delays, paperwork and conflicts between departments have increased.

As a project grows it is important to check that the structure and system supports the task rather than becomes an activity in itself. A useful technique is to track all the stages and people involved in a simple service or activity and see how it could be simplified or better managed. It is also worthwhile to see how the organisation could be designed around the user and the processes involved in meeting their needs rather than traditional specialist or professional boundaries.

Costing the project

New projects are often undercosted, either because project developers believe it will be easier to attract funds for a cheap project or because the full cost of operating is not known or not fully explored. Costing does require thorough work. Failing to identify costs or not including the full cost will usually create major problems.

A project's costs can be divided into:

■ recurring or non-recurring
■ directly related to the project, shared amongst other projects or indirect overheads
■ fixed or variable.

A manager of a health agency described her frustration about core costs,

'One of our main project funders gives out a very contradictory position about core costs. It is an upward battle to get them to contribute to the organisation's costs in managing, administrating and supporting the projects they sponsor. Yet at the same time they have become increasing concerned that we have sound and effective management, governance, organisational and financial control systems. How can they ask for such things and at the same time resist paying for them?'

Ways of approaching core costs

1 Reduce them down to a minimum level

Often organisations try to run down the costs involved in administrating the agency to the absolute minimum in the hope that funders might agree to fund a small element of the organisation's core costs.

The treasurer of a local development agency described how her organisation '...*almost prided ourselves on doing things on the cheap. In the past we took on projects that made very little or in some cases no contribution to the costs involved in running the agency. After a few years the consequence of this really began to show. Our management systems were poor. Staff had to spend time shoring up a creaking organisation – we have failed to invest in the organisational support systems needed to deliver the projects and services.'*

2 Ensure that costs are properly allocated within an agency

There is no universally accepted definition as to what is a core cost and what is a direct project cost. Most definitions draw a distinction between running the organisation's infrastructure and delivering services. One useful technique is to review how costs are apportioned. A youth agency found that several of the functions that made up its central costs could be regarded as direct costs. Issues such as facilitating user involvement, recruiting and training volunteers, project evaluation and publicity were regarded as core costs simply because they were activities that were co-ordinated from the agency's head office. The agency argued that many of these costs were integral to project delivery and so should be apportioned to the project's budget.

3 Seek specific funding for organisational capacity work

One strategy is to try to seek funding that is either unrestricted and can be used freely by the organisation or can be used to develop and support the organisation's structure – sometimes called capacity building. This funding is quite rare – most funders would prefer to pay for delivery than for administration. It might be available when an organisation is quite new, but is hard to secure long term.

4 Show how the core adds value to the project

Often organisations feel defensive about core costs. Funders imply that they have a duty to show that funding goes to the user rather than being swallowed up in running a bureaucracy. One approach is to tackle this head on by showing how the functions provided by the core costs – supervision, good management, quality assurance, policy work – all make a valuable input into the project and that without them the project would be weaker and less effective.

Recurring or non-recurring costs

Recurring costs are those you expect to incur as part of the project's regular cycle, for example electricity and telephones. The amount may vary, but the headings will probably be there every year.

Non-recurring costs are one-off costs. Projects usually incur two kinds of non-recurring costs – capital and start-up.

Capital costs

Capital costs cover expenditure on items you do not expect to incur every year, for example buildings and major equipment. Central and local government usually organise capital funding separately from annual revenue funding. Some capital items lose value over time. This is called 'depreciation'. You need to calculate how many years you think the capital item will last and divide this by the total cost to get a depreciation rate. For example, a car may cost £10,000. You estimate that it will last for five years. The car depreciates by £2,000 every year. If you are going to need a car permanently, you need to plan how to build up a fund to meet this capital expenditure in five years' time. Buying capital items usually also means annual expenditure on running costs and maintenance (i.e. recurring costs).

Start-up costs

Invariably a new project will incur some costs on one-off items of expenditure. These include costs of the start-up phase and the costs involved in launching a new organisation, for example recruitment and legal fees. These should not be recurring costs and need to be budgeted and accounted for separately. Start-up costs are often underestimated.

Costs directly related to the project, shared amongst other projects or indirect overheads

A project operating in or managed by an organisation can have three types of costs – direct, shared and indirect.

Direct costs

These are the costs exclusively incurred by the project. For example, if an environmental organisation set up a consultancy project, the costs of the project staff, their equipment, administration and running costs could all be regarded as direct costs dedicated to the project. The organisation is only paying for these items because it has set up the project.

Shared costs

It often makes economic sense for projects to share some costs. Examples include office space, administrative support and resources. The budget allocation for each project can be established by measuring actual usage, using an agreed formula based on the size of each project or simply dividing the shared costs by the number of operating projects.

Indirect costs

Indirect costs are the costs of being part of the bigger organisation. They include shared organisational costs, central management costs and charges. This expenditure is not directly related to costs of the project.

Sometimes an organisation describes the indirect costs (often together with the shared costs) as a management fee, which it charges to a project's budget.

In developing this approach to costing three things often happen:

- **The cost of the project is more than expected.** Often this happens because it is the first time the full costs have been identified. This may suggest that the full cost of operating a project has previously been underestimated. It might also be because an organisation that fully costs its work is unlikely to have many 'slush funds' to subsidise the real cost of operating.
- **Costs need justifying.** This process often causes a 'power shift' in organisations as people start to question if the amount paid in indirect costs is reasonable. Does the central management really 'add value' to the project or is the project having to carry a top heavy bureaucracy?
- **The way costs are allocated can be arbitrary.** There are no strict rules about what is a direct, shared or indirect cost. For example, one agency ran five local projects. The agency co-ordinator felt it was not right to regard all her salary as an indirect cost. Instead, she reviewed her time and came up with a breakdown of 40 per cent of her time being on the agency-wide issues (an indirect cost), 30 per cent time providing support and supervision to the projects (a shared cost) and 30 per cent split between two projects doing direct service delivery work (direct costs charged to the two projects).

Costing a project

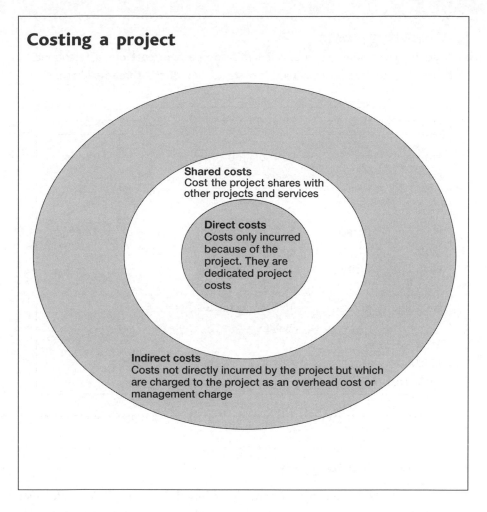

Shared costs
Cost the project shares with
other projects and services

Direct costs
Costs only incurred
because of the
project. They are
dedicated project
costs

Indirect costs
Costs not directly incurred by the project but which
are charged to the project as an overhead cost or
management charge

Allocating costs

A youth development agency used this approach to cost out a telephone counselling project. It allocated all costs to one of the three headings:

Direct project costs	Shared costs	Indirect costs
Project worker's salary	30% of info officer's salary	15% of director's salary
Help line costs	20% of agency office costs	15% of central costs
Help line volunteer costs	15% of training budget	15% of contingency costs
Help line publicity	15% of personnel budget	
Help line resources	15% of resources budget	
Start up costs		
£29,000	£14,000	£11,000
Total cost: £54,000		

Fixed or variable costs

Fixed costs are costs you incur regardless of how busy you are. Variable costs relate directly to usage. For example, a transport service will have to pay costs such as permanent staff wages, office rent and hire purchase on vehicles if it makes one or one hundred journeys a month, as these costs are fixed. Costs such as fuel and sessional staff are variable items. The project incurs these costs in direct relation to how busy it gets.

The relationship between fixed and variable costs is particularly important in estimating a break-even point for projects that charge for their work. This is the point at which the project has enough business to generate an income sufficient to cover its costs.

Current business thinking is to design organisations to be as flexible and as economic as possible by increasing the variable element through using sessional rather than permanent staff and buying in services from external suppliers when needed. The long-term effects and benefits of this strategy are not yet clear. It could be that increased use of variable items may be more costly and reduces morale within an organisation.

What's the real cost?

Morton Care Centre had been pleased with the progress of its negotiations with the social services department. It looked as if it would soon have a project up and running that would provide support and advice for carers. However, at the last minute the social services' business manager raised a problem. The project plan set out a detailed budget to employ a project co-ordinator, information officer and assistant, which totalled £78,000. The centre added on to this a further £9,360 to cover the management and administrative costs incurred by the Centre in managing, supporting and housing the centre.

The business manager felt that £9,360 was too high a management charge. Could it be broken down further? Did it provide best value?

The Centre's manager and treasurer set about trying to justify the management cost. This proved difficult until the treasurer had an idea. She explained that a judgement could only be made about the relevance of a cost if there was a relevant comparison. Her idea was to test the management fee against an alternative of setting up the project as an entirely independent body.

They set about costing the project as if it were an independent body and identified the following extra costs:

Cost	Amount
Regrading project co-ordinator to take into account extra management responsibilities	£1,500
Purchasing external non-management supervision for the project co-ordinator	£1,000
Independent fax line, e-mail and other office equipment	£500
Operating as an independent legal body – costs of training and supporting independent trustees	£500
Producing own annual report, publicity material and newsletter	£750
Having own resources, materials and library	£1,000
Obtaining independent specialist legal and financial advice	£750

Contracting out management services – e.g. payroll and
bookkeeping £1,250

Independent insurance cover £500

Employing part time receptionist/office assistant £6,500

Extra contingency costs £750

Total extra cost of being independent **£15,000**

Deducting the management cost of £9,360 would mean that the project
would cost £7,860 more to operate as an independent body.

The Centre's manager recognised that the budget did not take into account
two benefits of the project being part of the centre:

- **Time saved:** If the project was independent the co-ordinator would
  have to spend considerable time on managing the project, servicing the
  management committee and all the other tasks involved in running an
  independent body. This time (possibly as much as one day a week)
  would have to come from direct service delivery work with carers.
- **Gains:** By being part of the Centre the project would have direct access
  to the expertise, contacts and experience of the Centre's other staff.
  This would have a major impact on the project's performance as it
  would be able to draw from the strengths of being part of larger
  agency.

The Centre was able to argue that the management charge added value to
the project and provided it with an efficient and economic base.

Understanding the financial structure of the project

As well as working out the project's likely costs and sources of expenditure you
need to give thought to its financial structure or economy. There are four
important factors:

- The movement of money within the project.
- Patterns of cash flow.
- Pricing policies for money-making projects.
- The need for sensible reserves and contingency.

It is possible for a project to have problems with its finances even if the budget
balances. It is not just about the 'bottom line'. It is worth exploring the following
potential issues when setting up a project.

Start-up costs subsidise the first year

Often the enthusiasm for a new project means that funders can be quite generous at the start and provide money for the start-up. This is fine provided that the project does not rely upon start-up money to subsidise its running costs. One small project with a total income of £60,000 received a start-up budget of £12,000 in its first year. This was often used for recurring expenditure, and created serious financial problems in the second and third years.

Is the balance of costs right?

Is the balance between restricted and non-restricted income right? How do you make sure that all costs can be met? Can you justify the management and administration costs? There is no fixed rule about the appropriate ratio between direct project costs and expenditure on organisational management. Some organisations aim to keep management costs to between 15 and 20 per cent of the project's total costs. However, you can only make useful comparisons between projects if the same rules have been followed about direct, shared and indirect costs.

Are there any time lag problems?

Could a slow or a delayed start affect the project's income? It is usual for project expenditure to be high at the start. Could this cause a cash flow problem?

How and when will we have to replace capital items?

How long will our capital items really last? When do we need to replace them? How can we set aside a fund to do this?

Will there be sufficient uncommitted working capital?

Is there sufficient flexibility in the budget? Will we be able to follow up opportunities and use our cash intelligently?

Staffing the project

In all projects much of the project's success depends upon the quality and effectiveness of paid staff. Issues such as identifying the right skills, drawing up sound person specifications and job descriptions and managing the recruitment process are critical. Often they are rushed or entered into as a bureaucratic chore rather than a critical task.

Skills needed

As the project develops the skills needed change. Often commitment to the project's vision and values is seen as more important than getting the right skills. This is a hard issue. A commitment to or, at the very least, an understanding of the vision and values in a small project will probably be an essential requirement for all staff.

The balance of skills needed within a project change over the project's life span. A useful exercise is to think about the type of skills needed now and how they will change over time. Some will remain constant, others will become more or less important at different times.

One project working with special educational needs experienced problems between the skills they needed and the people they recruited. The treasurer described her experience:

'The job adverts and job descriptions were not properly considered. What we needed in the staff team were people able to negotiate funds, organise an office, influence statutory partners and run training for our volunteer workers. The job advert, job description and the discussion at interview was all about our philosophy and practice in educational needs. We recruited two very talented case workers and then effectively asked them to become project managers. We needed them to set the project up and recruit volunteers who would do the core work. One person was able to work out what was needed and adapt to this. The other hates doing anything but casework. He refuses to or is unable to do any project development work. It is our fault. We did not think clearly enough about what skills were needed.'

Different skills for different times

A project needs to use the available skills of its staff and supporters throughout its life. Specific skills needed change during particular phases. The trick is to make sure that the project keeps encouraging the right people with the right skills to take a lead at a particular time, and possibly to back off when their skills are not so central to the project's current needs.

The skill mix needed in a project can change quite rapidly as the project moves into new phases. Raising funds and setting up a service need different skills from those needed to supervise, train and support a staff team.

In a review of two three-year projects it was possible to identify how the skills need of the project changed:

Innovation
- Vision building
- Creative thinking
- Group development and facilitation

Definition
- Skills in strategy
- Planning and design

Testing
- Analytical skills

Building support
- Influencing
- Marketing
- Fundraising

Designing and planning
- Costing and budgeting
- Planning
- Management

The launch
- Team development
- Marketing

The operational phase
- Management
- Team leadership
- Skills in delivery
- Communication

The project's closure
- Organisational skills
- Evaluation skills
- Strategic skills

In reality no project has the ability to turn people and their skills on and off as needed, but this sort of skill profiling does raise several issues about team development, staffing and project leadership.

One project was led by the person who had the big idea to set the project up. She was brilliant at communicating the vision, making deals with funders and getting things going. Somehow she assumed the position of project director. Once the project was up and running it needed to create systems and develop services. The director did not like to spend time on such mundane and bureaucratic activities. She preferred having ideas rather than turning them into long-term, workable solutions. It was not until she left the post that the project was able to recruit a new person to lead the project into its mainstream phase.

What would have happened if she had not left? Would the project have failed to develop? How could the project steering group have ensured that she recognised her role had to change within the project? How could they have helped her to learn or develop new skills?

Skills audits, staff and committee appraisals, staff development and open discussion about strengths and weaknesses can help a project recognise and plan what skills it needs to take it onto its next phase.

Managing a fixed-term project

It is useful to distinguish between a project whose main funds are renewed every year and one designed with a specific end date. Most statutory authorities grant aid or contract for a fixed time. Many projects exist on an annual cycle in which they apply for funds every year. Increasingly many organisations are now developing fixed-term projects, which they do not envisage becoming permanent. Given the uncertainty of annually renewable projects, fixed-term projects need to think very carefully about how they design and manage a time limited piece of work.

Broadly speaking there are three main approaches to planning time limited projects:

- **Ignore the time limit.** Work on the basis that the project will be so good and so successful that funding will turn up to continue it and make it permanent. A high risk and somewhat reckless strategy.
- **Manage it with the end in mind.** Develop contingency plans and ideas in case the project closes, but manage it as if it is an ongoing entity. If funding does dry up then, with time, the project should be able to extricate itself.

- **Design the project with a clear end point.** Work on the basis that the project should be fixed-term and will terminate. It could be replaced by a permanent or new short-term project, but its role is to stimulate and innovate change within a fixed period.

Badly managing a fixed-term project or ignoring the reality until it is too late can cause major problems:

- **Suddenly or badly planned withdrawal.** People with whom the project works or who benefit from its services continue to need and expect them. Sudden or badly planned withdrawal can create massive problems for service users and communities. They are left 'high and dry'. In some cases it might have been better not to have offered the service in the first place.
- **Staff uncertainty.** Staff feel uncertain and insecure as they wait to hear if the project is to be extended or renewed. Their performance and enthusiasm wane. The project's focus shifts from doing the work to survival and funding. It falls into short-term crisis management and diverts energy into scrabbling around for short-term funding. There is no vision, direction or planning beyond that of getting funding. Many projects have been damaged through losing key people to more secure posts in the final phases of the project.

The following are important when designing and planning effective fixed-term projects.

Sustainability

If the project is to run for two years what will be there in three years' time? What part of the project's legacy could happen without the project? Some aspects of sustainability will be tangible, such as buildings or resources, others such as new skills learnt or better practice being followed, are intangible. An unsustainable project is one that leaves a gap when it stops. People need it and expect it to be there. They cannot operate without its support and management.

Focus on the end point

A useful technique is to develop a vision of how you would like things to be at the end of the project and then work backwards. This type of scenario planning is a useful way of clarifying what kind of outcomes the project needs to achieve. The end of the project should be seen as the main target and all of the project's activities should lead up to that.

Develop a staff team that is geared around the end point

People applying for jobs with the project need to know that it will be fixed-term. They will need support and practical help to find other work when the project closes. Secondment – from within or outside the organisation – is one way of helping to overcome job insecurity.

End on a high point

Do not let the project fade out. Make sure plans are made to record and disseminate its experiences. Make sure that the project's achievements will be identified, acknowledged and celebrated. This process needs to start early.

Developing an 'exit strategy'

Exit strategies are not easy. At times it is tempting to suggest that an exit strategy is a new concept used to make short-term funding sound more intelligent and effective than it actually is. It implies that everything can be planned and managed to order. All the project has to do is set itself up, do its work and then move into its prepared exit strategy. However, if projects are to be short-term, serious thought needs to be given to what happens when the project, or its own sources of funding, cease.

Increasingly exit strategies are requested by funders when funding or project bids are being considered. At this stage it is difficult to prove that the exit strategy will work. All you can show is that you have thought about it intelligently and have developed some plans. How the project closes down and what happens to its work is a question that needs to be reviewed at key milestones throughout its life.

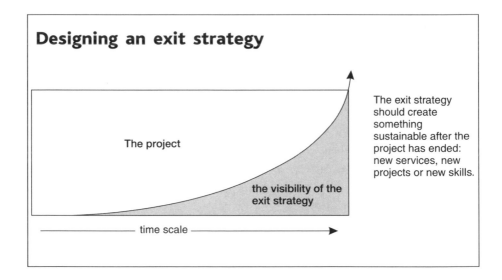

Designing an exit strategy

The project

the visibility of the exit strategy

time scale

The exit strategy should create something sustainable after the project has ended: new services, new projects or new skills.

Choosing your exit

Possible strategy	Example	Issues	Potential problems	Action needed
The project becomes permanent and self-supporting	An agency secured funding for a community café with the plan that after two years it would be able to generate income to be a viable community business.	Need to develop a business plan projecting the full costs involved in being self-supporting and the actions and support needed to become viable.	Often the true costs involved in being self-supporting are not fully recognised or known.	Need to monitor costs continually and revise projections and assumptions about what is needed to be independent.
The project is a one off	A charity ran a anti bullying project with three schools – it made it clear from the start that it would only operate for two years and not be a permanent resource.	Important to be clear from the outset that the project is only temporary to avoid people becoming dependent on it.	Some cynicism from some people about 'what is the point of another short-term project that will vanish onto thin air?'	The project must make it clear to all users, partners and others that it not be a permanent feature. Only take on what you can fully deliver.
The project is a demonstration project	A homeless agency ran an innovative project tackling youth homelessness. It built in research and evaluation time to demonstrate learning from the project in the hope that others would take it up.	Costs of research, evaluation and dissemination must be built in to the project. Often demonstration projects need time to show that they have been effective.	Good research and evaluation takes time, can be costly and requires independence. Danger of just producing another glossy report to sit on the shelf.	Need to plan the research and dissemination project from the start.

Possible strategy	Example	Issues	Potential problems	Action needed
The project creates partners	A health promotion project built up a network of teachers, nurses and others who could continue the work on after the project had ceased.	The project needs to ensure that the partners have the skills, support and organisation to carry on the work.	The partners might feel that they are being pushed into taking the project on. Do they have the time and capacity?	The project must put time into building up a network of partners.
The project scales down its activities towards the end	A specialist advice agency implemented a close down plan – it stopped taking on new cases six months before the project was due to end.	Needs the discipline of saying 'no'. The project may also need to plan what happens to staff and other resources during the close down.	The close down needs careful management – it can be a depressing affair!	Need to have dates agreed in advance at which to implement the close down plan.
Follow up projects and activities are created	A neighbourhood community development project created volunteer-based community groups to carry on the work and obtained resources to support the follow on.	The project should see its key role as building the capacity for all the follow up activities.	Will the spin off projects be able to operate without the project's input and support?	The project must give the lead to help the follow on activities develop.
Aim for another funder to take over funding	When its three year lottery funded project ends a carers support project hopes the local authority will take over funding.	The project must understand other funders' lead times.	Funders can be reluctant to take over another funder's project; they often prefer 'new' projects.	The project must get early support from potential follow on funders. Does it need to be reinvented in order to attract new support?

The following are examples of strategies that can be used to make the project's work sustainable.

- **The project becomes permanent and self supporting.** It moves onto another stage. It is able to generate income from its activities or raise income from sources other than those that supported it in its first phase.
- **The project is a one off.** No follow up is necessary as the project is planned to be unique. It can end without creating needs or leaving people expecting more.
- **The project is a demonstration project.** The project must decide how it will disseminate and share its experience with others who may decide to run other projects as a result. It must help others to learn from them by documenting and sharing its experiences through training, reports, events and consultancy.
- **The project creates partners.** The project identifies key groups and individuals who will be able to carry on its work after it has ceased. The partners will need resources, support and early involvement in the project if they are to be successful.
- **The project scales down its activities towards the end.** It only takes on work it can finish within the time available. All work must therefore have a clear completion date.
- **Follow up projects and activities are created.** The project sets up and secures resources for spin-off projects and activities that should be able to operate independently when the project has ceased.
- **Another funder takes over the funding.** The project works to get another funder to take over the funding once the initial funding has ended.

A bad ending

A manager of a health agency described her frustration about core costs,

Morton Leisure Development Project was a well planned and designed initiative. Its programme of health education and sports participation was well received, innovative and filled a long-standing gap. It had secure funds for three years. Discussion of what would happen after the three years had been tactfully avoided.

Towards the end of the second year the project staff started to express concern about the future. A fundraising consultant was engaged to look at how the project could be funded in the long term. Approaches to possible funders were disappointing. They all recognised the project's useful and creative work. Funders would like to find a way to help but there was little if any possibility of long-term or core funding. The best on offer would be occasional bits of project funding.

In the third year the tone and style of the project changed. The project leader spent most of her time looking for alternative income to continue the project. Staff felt demoralised and worried about their prospects. The level of work remained roughly the same, but the project lacked the spark it once had. All energy and attention went into chasing after funding rather than developing the work.

Four months before the end of the project the staff and steering group realised there was little chance of the project continuing after the three years. The best option would be to use some local authority underspend to delay the closure for a few months.

The project faded away in its final six months. Some staff left early. There was little enthusiasm and excitement about any of its activities. The impending closure loomed large.

Eighteen months on the project is forgotten. People have a vague memory of there having been something about health and sport. Indeed, there is now talk of creating a small project to do similar work.

The former project leader made the following observations:

■ 'We denied reality. From the outset no promise or indication was made that there would be or could be any long-term funding. We ignored that and got carried away by our own enthusiasm. We organised our activities as if they would go on for ever. It would have been better if, at the start, we had said what lasting difference five people with three years' funding could make. We should have seen ourselves as pilots and developers rather than mainstream providers. We made the mistake of thinking like an organisation and not like a project. We wanted to be a permanent entity rather than focusing on creating change.

■ We should have worked towards the end. The hardest kind of fundraising is to go to someone and say 'our initial funding is about to run out. We will soon be out of work. We would like you to pick up the tab'. It is hardly a positive or enticing pitch. We should have put together a programme of spin off projects, new activities and other initiatives that could have grown out of the main project.

■ We should have ended on a high. It is hard to remember it now, but for the first two years the project was a huge success. It was dynamic and made a real impact locally. We lost it. We turned inwards and became focused on securing the non-existent holy grail of permanent funding. Once we took our eye off the ball we lost it.'

Managing the exit

For any of the above exit strategies to work the project must, from the start, be:

- **Outcome focused.** Everyone in the project must see the end point as being critical. All the project's activities and work must come together. The outcomes should be identifiable, sustainable and not reliant on the project's staff.
- **Skilled at building alliances.** Usually exit strategies depend on others. Other people are needed to take the work on, to fund, resource and support it. The project must be skilled at transferring the project to the people who will take it on.
- **Skilled at managing change.** The project needs to be focused on creating identifiable change. It needs to involve other people in implementing the exit strategy. It must be able to hand over its work, ideas and vision to others.
- **Firm with itself.** The project needs to be disciplined. It must avoid taking on activities and commitments that it will not be around to see through or finish properly. It has to keep to the project plan however tempting departures from it might seem.

Designing the project checklist

Has your project:

- ☐ Developed a supportive structure?

- ☐ Identified the different types of costs involved?

- ☐ Planned its likely cash flow?

- ☐ Recognised the full organisational costs involved in managing the project?

- ☐ Recognised the different kinds of skills needed at different points?

- ☐ Planned what will happen when it ends?

- ☐ Agreed possible exit strategies?

chapter 8

GETTING THE PROJECT ORGANISED

This chapter looks at:

- Developing a project plan
- Drawing up the first budget
- Drawing up an initial business plan
- Recruiting staff
- Planning the project's launch

Once you have made decisions about the project's design there will be considerable work involved to get the project ready. All the activities require hard work, often to tight deadlines. In many respects what happens to the project is determined in the detail. Decisions about legal structures, budgets, costs and personnel will have much more impact on the project's chance of success than time spent drafting vision statements.

Developing a project plan

Planning the start-up phase

This phase needs to bring together, clearly and logically, all the tasks that need to be done and the decisions that need to be made. The plan should be produced so that it:

- Sets out all the tasks and decisions involved in a clear and measurable way.
- Matches available human and other resources with the tasks.
- Produces an easy to monitor plan that lets you note and record progress.
- Highlights any departure from the plan at an early stage so that remedial action can be taken quickly to overcome delays, blocks or problems.
- Produces key milestones to which those involved in the project work.

Quite often new projects are being set up against the clock. A deadline has been agreed and the plan needs to ensure that all the start-up activities can be carried out so that it can start on time. Examples of against the clock projects include when a funder has money to spend by a certain date (usually the end of the financial year) or when there is a pressing political or other reason that determines when the project must start. In such cases the start-up plan must balance expediency and realism. Individuals managing this phase need to know that the tasks can be carried out in a sound manner. Failure to do so can lead to the project being bounced into commitments and promises that it struggles to meet, or being set up to fail.

A simple planning framework is based around three key elements:

1 Starting at the end point and working backwards.
2 Identifying key milestones towards the end points.
3 Scheduling in and resourcing tasks and decisions to achieve each milestone.

Established project planning techniques

Project management as a branch of management studies has its main roots in the defence and engineering industries. Several techniques and systems have been drawn up to manage and plan complex projects. They all contain the following elements:

- Listing and estimating all the activities involved.
- Noting any dependent relationship between activities (e.g. activity x can only happen after activity y has been completed).
- Putting the activities into a logical order.
- Calculating the shortest time to get through all the activities in a logical fashion.

There are three main techniques:

- **Critical Path Model.** A critical path is a method of calculating the duration of all the tasks involved in a project by estimating each task, linking it to others and working out the optimum route (the critical path) through from start to finish.
- **Programme Evaluation Review Technique (PERT).** PERT was developed in the 1950s by the United States Navy to schedule large projects. Similar to a critical path analysis a PERT chart (sometimes called a network diagram) sets out in graphic form the relationships between tasks and the overall likely duration.
- **Gantt chart.** A Gantt chart (named after Henry L Gantt) sets out different tasks on a bar chart across a time scale. The strength of a Gantt chart is its graphic representation and the ability to track progress quickly.

- These techniques have a mixed reputation. They do provide a useful discipline, can help to get things in order and can identify potential problems or delays. However, there is a tendency for them to become over complex and jargonistic. To use the technique properly all the details about time scales, deadlines and availability need to be clear at the start of the project. There is also a tendency for planners to assume that everything works in a logical fashion.

- Plans and planning tools need to be active and flexible. They should not be regarded as shackles that tie down the project's development. Plans need to be reviewed and reshaped in the light of experience and developments. Effective and regular monitoring of the plan is vital.

Drafting a project plan

Barnwick Community Trust used a traditional project planning technique to organise its one year pilot project to support the work of new and developing community groups. During the year the Trust's team would make contact with interested parties, carry out a needs study, work with six pilots, evaluate the work and develop funding bids for new projects.

The project planning technique allowed the team to break the project into manageable chunks and then to schedule the whole project.

The final project plan set out each key task with a box

estimated start date   *estimated finish date*

lead responsibility   *days needed*

The plan made clear the project's very tight timetable. It also showed the key phases of the work.

It also helped the team to monitor progress, identify milestones and ensure that the project kept on track.

Critical path plan

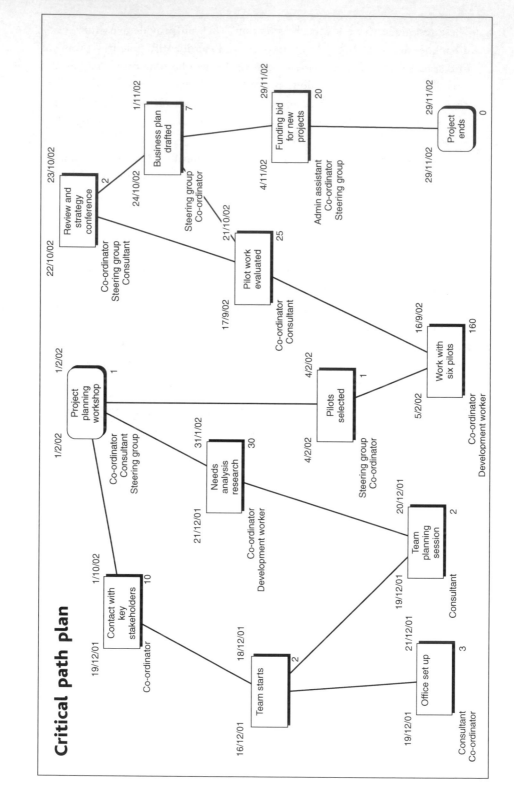

Planning your project

This simple planning tool has three main aims:

1 To help participants understand the entire project by breaking it down into tasks and then building it up into a timed plan.
2 To identify the main tasks involved in delivering the project.
3 To spot key milestones and identify the minimum time needed to deliver the project.

Example: a project to consult the residents of a local area about priorities for their estate

Stage 1	Task	Time	Resources	Lead
Generate a list of all the different tasks that you anticipate being involved in the project. For each task allocate responsibility (i.e. who is responsible for making it happen), resources needed and the estimated time needed to deliver the task. Once all the tasks have been agreed transfer them onto post-it notes.	Design survey	3 days		Researcher
	Organise public meeting	7 days	Room Budget Speakers	Project leader Volunteers

Stage 2

The next stage is to organise the task. Draw a line from start to finish and put each task in a logical order. Spot 'dependencies' – tasks that can only be done if other tasks have been done first.

```
┌─────────┐       ┌─────────┐       ┌─────────┐
│ Collate │  ───▶ │ Analyse │  ───▶ │ Write   │
│ survey  │       │ responses│       │ report  │
│ responses│      └─────────┘       └─────────┘
└─────────┘            │                  ▲
                       ▼                  │
                  ┌──────────┐            │
                  │ Brief    │ ───────────┘
                  │ steering │
                  │ group    │
                  └──────────┘

                              ┌──────────┐
                              │ Prepare  │
                              │ feedback │
                              │ sessions │
                              └──────────┘
```

Stage 3

Analyse the plan:

- How much time will it take to get from the start to the end?
- Are there any obvious milestones – when the project goes from one stage to another?
- Are there any obvious decision points in the life of the project?
- Are there any points of overload in the plan – for example too many tasks taking place at one time or too much depending on one person?
- Is there a need for some slack or contingency time?
- Once the plan has been agreed it is possible to draw up a workplan for each individual or group involved in the project, making it clear when they will be needed.

Drawing up the first budget

As the project moves towards its launch, work will need to be given to its first budget. This must be able to do the following:

- Ensure that the project is able to function and has sufficient income to match likely expenditure.
- Provide a control system for finance and sufficient space for flexibility.
- Ensure that the project has sufficient management information available to plan and monitor.

In the past all that really concerned treasurers and finance people was the bottom line: making sure that income met expenditure. Budgeting was a balancing act. This is changing fast. Many organisations are changing the format of their budgets. In the past it has been hard to establish from some budgets and accounts exactly what was spent on particular activities as budget headings were mainly a product of administrative convenience or history. Expenditure was grouped together in broad headings such as salaries or administration.

Nowadays organisations are moving to budgets that show more accurately the full cost of a particular activity or project.

As funding for projects is more tightly managed, funders and purchasers want to know what a project costs. They are unwilling to fund an organisation in the hope that funds will trickle down into the project in which they are interested. There is a growing concern that some organisations spend too much on administration and management and not enough on their primary activity.

This means that projects need to be much clearer about the operating costs and the make up in the budget. Some organisations underestimate the cost of operating. This has led to impoverished organisations that can be criticised for 'always doing things on the cheap'.

About budgets

The budget is a statement of intent. Budgets must be related to objectives or strategy and not simply about balancing income and expenditure. The budget is the organisation's most deliberate statement of strategy and priorities.

Strategy not finance led

The budget should follow your strategy, not dictate it. It is important that the budget setting exercise is firmly led by your plans and priorities.

Create flexibility

Good budgeting should allow some room for flexibility, new developments and opportunities.

Not fixed in stone

A useful practice is periodically to rebuild the budget as if you were starting again. This practice, called 'zero based budgeting', requires you to review all items and ensure that spending levels are in line with your priorities. It stops the common practice of building all the budget around past patterns rather than what you want to do in the future.

Start-up costs

It is common to underestimate a project's start-up costs. In the rush to get the project going key activities are undercosted or overlooked. The following checklist shows the most common start-up areas:

People costs

Recruitment costs can be high. You may need to include additional funds to cover staff and volunteer training and temporary staff costs.

Premises costs

Careful budgeting is needed to plan for and control legal fees (such as negotiating leases), move-in expenses and insurance costs. It is worth spending time researching the likely costs of bringing new accommodation up to a reasonable and safe standard, as well as the costs of extra fittings, furniture and additional security. The costs of improving access to the premises need to be included in the project costs.

Operating costs

Include the cost of buying items such as computers, software, stationery and office materials as well as the cost of any vehicle purchase.

Business costs

Two business costs need careful forecasting:

- **Slow start costs** – Often new income generating projects have to build up a level of business. Their income will therefore be smaller in the first few months.
- **Cash flow costs** – If a project spends proportionally more of its annual budget at the start of the year but receives its income equally throughout the year it

will have a cash flow problem. The costs of meeting the cash flow gap (such as through a bank loan) need to be planned.

Launch costs

Remember to include the costs involved in designing publicity materials and organising the project's launch.

Cash flow

It should be possible to sketch out the likely pattern of cash flow within the project for the first year. It is difficult to be exact about cash flow, but at this stage of a project's development any negative cash flow needs identifying. There are three common problems:

- A project may not earn much income in its start-up phase because not all its activities are up and running or because take up is low.
- The project costs are likely to be greater at the start of the year while income is spread evenly throughout the year.
- The payment patterns of your main income sources are retrospective or prone to lateness.

Any significant cash flow problem needs to be identified and resolved or the cost of managing cash flow built into the cost of the project.

Pricing policy

Increasingly projects are having to charge for their services. Determining a pricing policy is a critical issue in the project's business plan. To do it effectively you must have sound and reliable information about the cost of an activity. Costing should be an objective and rational exercise based on the relationship between different types of cost. Pricing is a much more tactical exercise.

The following points need attention.

What is the break even point?

The break even point is the point at which your total income is equal to the total costs of the activity.

For example, the fixed costs of training project are £300 per week and each trainee brings in a contract worth £45. The variable cost of each trainee such as equipment is £10. The break even point would be reached at nine trainees. Pricing strategies need to be based around achieving a viable break even point. When the break even point is reached the project has (at its current level of operation) covered its main fixed costs.

The break even point

Number of trainees	Fixed cost	Variable cost	Total cost	Income	Profit (−loss)
12	300	120	420	540	120
11	300	110	410	495	85
10	300	100	400	450	50
9	**300**	**90**	**390**	**405**	**15**
8	300	80	380	360	−20
4	300	40	340	180	−160
2	300	20	320	90	−230
0	300	0	300	0	−300

The break point

Number of trainees	Fixed cost	Variable cost	Total cost	Income	Profit (−loss)
17	550	170	720	765	45
16	550	160	710	720	10
15	550	150	700	675	−25
14	**550**	**140**	**690**	**630**	**−60**
13	300	130	430	585	155
12	300	120	420	540	120
11	300	110	410	495	85
10	300	100	400	450	50
9	300	90	390	405	15

The project would reach a point where it could not take any more trainees without taking on more staff, expanding its base and possibly allowing the indirect costs to increase. In this example, we will assume that the project hits the 'break point' at around 14 trainees. It needs more staff and other resources, which are fixed costs. So it decides that in order to continue expanding (it could have chosen to say no ...) its fixed costs have to rise by £250 per week.

In this case the decision to increase fixed costs means that the project starts to make a loss. It needs to be confident that this is only a temporary loss and that it will soon be able to attract more trainees.

Identifying and managing the break even and break points is tricky. Often projects have more than one or two break points. Some, such as the level of supervision or admin support, may not be easy to quantify as a number. Operating at or beyond the break point can cause stress and is likely to reduce the quality and responsiveness of what you do.

The break even point is critical in projects dependent on a unit or fee-based income. The break point is relevant in all projects that have to cope with demand and need to plan how best they can respond.

How does the market work?

Any feasibility study or business plan would need to have considered the price sensitivity of the market. What do similar and related providers charge? Who sets the price? What will the market pay for? How stable is it?

Avoid loss leaders

A loss leader is a deliberately low price set with the intention of enticing customers. Once they are in you hope that they like it so much they will stay loyal to you as you raise your prices. Loss leaders are highly risky. Often all they do is create an expectation that the service is cheap.

How will the purchase be structured?

Can you reward purchasers for providing you with the security of a block purchase? Unit or spot based contracts often cost more. The organisation providing the service has to take a gamble that it might not reach its break even point. It builds an element to cover the cost of this risk into its fee.

The need for sensible reserves and contingency

A controversial issue in the voluntary sector is to what level and for what purposes charities should build up reserves. On the one hand, some people would argue that it is wrong to let money sit in a bank account when it could be being used for its intended purpose. On the other hand, sound financial management would stress the need to cover problems, manage cash flow and emergencies and follow up opportunities. The Charity Commission has published a paper suggesting that reserves covering between two and twenty-four months' operating costs are reasonable. Each organisation needs to establish its own reserves policy based on the possible risks and the need for effective planning. You should give careful thought at the start of a project to ensuring such a fund can be built up.

Management information

At the start of the project decide what sort of financial monitoring and reporting system will be needed. This is a sensible thing to do in any organisation but is particularly important with a new project. The first year needs careful monitoring to check that the actual performance of the budget is in line with your original plans. If it starts to vary significantly then you should take early action and decisions.

Drawing up an initial business plan

A business plan is an organisation 'setting out its stall'. It is a public statement of the project's overall aims, direction, management and financial plans. Detailed advice on business planning is contained in my book *The Complete Guide to Business and Strategic Planning* (Lawrie, 2001). Several parts of the plan will have already been worked on in earlier stages of the project's development.

The main headings for a business plan for a new project are:

- **A summary page.** A one page outline of the main points. This would be similar in content to the project outline.
- **Introduction and mission.** A brief introduction to the plan with a short statement setting out the vision and values that are central to the project.
- **The background.** A short review of the history that led up to the creation of the project. This should also summarise the need for the project. If the project is part of or is sponsored by an existing organisation include details of the organisation.
- **A review.** A brief commentary on the main issues with which the project will deal. This should include a description of the need for the project, the gap it will fill and the opportunities open to it.
- **Future trends.** A description of the main developments and trends the project anticipates. Will demand for it rise? What political, organisational and social changes need to be taken into account? You will need to show evidence that the project has thought about likely changes to the environment in which it operates.
- **The strategy for the project.** A comprehensive outline of the project's main priorities. What will its focus be? Specific, measured and timed objectives can be included to spell out the detail of what the project will do.
- **Implications.** What sort of organisation is needed to deliver the project? This would include a brief description of intended staffing, legal and management arrangements.

- **Financial implications.** An outline description of the financial assumptions on which the project is based, the costs involved and estimated income needed.
- **Track record.** Evidence that the people involved are able to deliver the project.

The following six points are important in a new project's business plan.

Show that it has been thought through

A good business plan shows that a project has been founded upon sensible assumptions and forecasts. It needs to set out the principles and conclusions of your thinking rather than detailed plans and budgets. People reading the plan should be able to understand quickly the rationale and 'big idea' behind the project.

Honesty and openness

A business plan needs to show that you have thought about and analysed potential risks or problems, and developed a strategy to deal with them. A business plan that attempts to 'gloss over' any risks or problems is unlikely to convince potential backers.

Don't predict what you don't know

Many commercial business plans are inclined to be dominated by detailed attempts to forecast future cash flow, budgets and performance. This is often a pointless exercise as the actual results rely on unknown circumstances and developments. In the first year of a project it may be possible to set out detailed plans. In the years that follow it is probably only feasible to estimate cautiously broad trends and developments.

Keep it active and short

With business plans it seems that the longer the document the more likely it is to be incoherent, imprecise and vague. It needs to be written in language focused on results. It has to be specific and clear. It is a working document that guides action rather than a policy paper of how we would like things to be.

It is more than a document

All too often organisations and projects produce plans that are never referred to again. After initial circulation they are filed away and forgotten about. A good business plan needs to set out a strategy for a project in such a way that people in and around the project will understand it and use the plan as a guide. The plan must be measurable. Progress in achieving the plan must be monitored on a regular basis.

Focus on the main messages

A useful exercise is to identify the main messages and ensure that the plan highlights them. The plan can probably only deal with three to five main messages. The section on strategy and the executive summary must set out clearly the main issues leading up to the project and the overall direction behind the plan.

Recruiting staff

It is interesting to note just how little time goes into recruiting staff in organisations compared with other decisions. Key appointments are often made on the basis of a 40 minute interview, whereas much less significant decisions are researched, tested and debated.

> One manager commented that it amazed him that
>
> *'we spent a day interviewing and selecting candidates for the critical post of project leader. We actually spent much more time agreeing which contractors would equip and paint the project office.'*

Most job descriptions are written to prevent disputes about whose job it is to do a particular task or to secure a pay grading. They are often long lists of possible tasks and responsibilities. They rarely convey a sense of the job's critical issues or the balance of skills needed. In the main they are an administrative tool. To get a way from this one American organisation now hires project managers on a one line job description – 'do what ever is legally needed to make the project a success'.

Increasingly, as part of good employment practice, many organisations also produce a person specification setting out the essential and desirable skills and knowledge areas (sometimes called competencies) needed in the job. The job description and the person specification are important and need careful attention.

In designing a job the following features need to be clear:

- What responsibilities are delegated to the postholder?
- What resources does the postholder manage?
- What decision making powers will she/he have?
- How will the postholder know she/he is being successful?
- What are the key success factors for the job? What are the main priorities?

- What key processes are involved?
- What are the outputs and outcomes?
- What will be expected of the postholder?
- What skills are needed?
- What are the key relationships within the job?
- Who are the key people with whom the postholder must work effectively? (This could include the importance of teamwork within the project.)
- How might changes to the job occur?

You may consider adding in a requirement that the postholder is committed to developing new skills and developing as the project changes.

Several organisations have experimented with producing a full job description for personnel and formal reasons and a working document such as a workplan to reflect job priorities at a given time. One agency sends out a one-page list of the key priority areas for the applicant if they were to be appointed. It lists the core tasks needed rather than possible functions and responsibilities.

The primary method of recruitment, the job interview, is an incredibly flawed and faulty way of making an important decision. Interviews are often subjective; they rely upon the skills of the interviewers to ask the right questions and to hold back from making subjective judgements. Some people would argue that all an interview really tells you is how good an individual can perform at a job interview. With this in mind the following points can help to strengthen the recruitment process:

Make it as objective a process as possible

Do all you can to remove the subjective elements. Design the recruitment tests around a clear person specification that lists the essential knowledge and skills areas needed. Work out a format for interviews that will apply to all candidates. Make a list of the areas which you need to test or find out about and ensure that you have prepared questions that will reveal what you need to know.

Work with the panel

Make sure everyone involved with recruitment and selection has had some basic training in the processes and skills involved and on issues concerning illegal direct and indirect employment discrimination. All panel members should apply the same criteria throughout the process.

Gather information and then make a judgement

See the process in two parts. The first should be about gathering information to test candidates against the person specification. The second should be about making judgements concerning their ability do the job as described. Often poor interviewers reverse this process. They make a snap judgement (often based on first impressions) and then spend the rest of the interview looking for evidence to support it.

Use other techniques

Other recruitment techniques can back up and support the interview. Those commonly used include presentations, practical tests and exercises, group discussion, psychological tests/profiles and written tests. All need careful planning and need to be related to the skills and experience that you have identified to do the job.

Don't rush the decision

Spend time checking that the job description and person specification really reflect what you want. Plan the interview carefully and be prepared to use second interviews or to readvertise if you are not confident that you can make a good selection.

Planning the project's launch

The launch of the project should be an opportunity to develop its identity, create goodwill towards it and consolidate the networks of support developed during the start-up period.

In planning the launch think about how you will design and develop an appropriate and effective public identity for the project. This is often difficult. You can be so close to a project that it is hard to think about it as if you were new to it. One law centre forgot to mention in its publicity material that it was both a free service and independent of local and central government. Both points were cornerstones of the centre's values. They were so obvious to the people in the project that they overlooked them.

There is also a danger of overselling a new project and promising too much. It is easy to set a project up as a panacea that will solve all known problems. If people believe that they will surely be quickly disappointed. In the launch stage it is sensible to indicate what the project cannot do as well as what it can do. One health project produced a simple leaflet to launch its services. On one side it said what it could do, on the other it listed things that it could not. The latter list is just as informative, if not more so, than the first. It helps to develop a realistic expectation of what can and cannot be done.

In planning the launch it is worthwhile to work out the main messages you want to get across. Try these out on people not connected to the project. Are you using appropriate language? Is it riddled with technical language, initials and jargon that only insiders know? Does it convey what is unique about the project?

The launch should provide an occasion to consolidate goodwill towards the project by thanking people who have helped out in the start-up phase. It is also useful for making them feel part of the project as it goes mainstream.

Getting the project organised checklist

Has your project:

☐ Agreed a project plan setting out all the key decisions and tasks?

☐ Assigned responsibility for delivering the plan?

☐ Recognised the start-up costs involved in the project?

☐ Developed a business plan setting out the project's strategy and action plan?

☐ Planned how to recruit the project's staff?

☐ Planned the project's launch?

chapter 9

KEY MANAGEMENT ISSUES

This chapter looks at:

- Keeping the project focused on its long-term vision
- The changing role of the management committee
- Moving the project on
- Managing the project's closure

A project's first year is a critical period. During this time real life takes over. Objectives, goals and plans are determined by practice and circumstance rather than by how we would like to see things. Power and decisions shift from those who plan to those who do. Patterns and expectations are built up.

Keeping the project focused on its long-term vision

Often in projects people assume that issues such as vision and values are clear to everyone involved. The assumption is held so strongly that no one takes responsibility for checking there is a central unity of purpose and ethos.

In one relatively new agency 13 staff, committee members and volunteers were asked to write down why they existed and what they believed was important about how the project operated. The statements were vastly different. For example, some thought the project's aim was to campaign against some of the local authority's policies. Others thought its role was to develop long-term partnerships and close relations with the authority. Many of the conflicts and uncertainties which the project experienced were identified as being linked to the lack of an agreed vision rather than personality clashes. The person who set up the project and chaired the committee was surprised at how little unity there was within the project. She recognised an urgent need to redefine exactly what the project was about.

The case of the lost vision

The coordinator of an environmental project used his skills as a systems engineer to describe how his project lost its way.

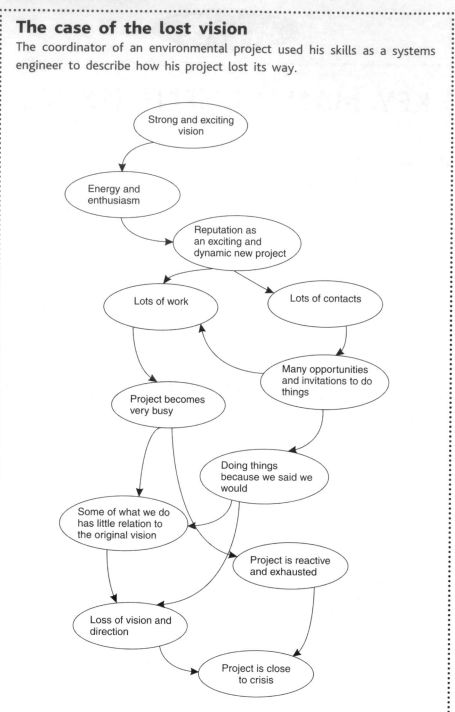

Looking back he describes the project's first 18 months.

'When we launched we felt very positive. There was enormous support and goodwill for the project. Lots of people and agencies were keen to work with us. We did not see it at the time, but we became swamped by work and contacts.

'We took on far too much. We allowed ourselves to become involved in many different types of meetings and potential projects.

'We were soon being driven by being busy rather than by what we wanted to do. At first it felt good to be busy. But soon we were too busy to think. We became reactive. We only did things when it was the last minute and was urgent.

'We are now trying to get out of the crisis that we have created. We have to make sure that we are in the driving seat and are strategic about what work we take on. We need to develop good monitoring and evaluation systems to help us to question our work. We need to become skilled at saying "no" and refusing to be bounced from idea to idea. Over the past six months we have been driven by urgency and activity rather than vision and direction. We must take action to restore it.'

Management committees have a particularly crucial role in safeguarding and promoting the project's vision and direction. As well as their legal and constitutional obligations they can have a useful vantage point to observe the project and evaluate its development. The committee is a part of the organisation, yet it is unlikely to be involved in the detailed day to day work. One popular way of describing its role is that it should focus on steering the direction and leave the rowing to the project staff.

The committee needs periodically to discuss the original vision that led to the project being set up. Useful prompts include:

- Is the vision still relevant?
- Are we making progress towards our vision?
- Is our strategy and planning work clearly influenced by our vision?

The vision should hold the project together and give it a sense of purpose. Often details and practicalities can weaken its significance. Pressure from funding bodies, new opportunities, organisational requirements and needs can all make the vision seem idealistic and remote. It has to be backed up with a strong and realistic strategy. But good strategy and sound management is not enough. Without a clear sense of vision or purpose the project will drift and achieve little.

Keeping the project under review

	Frequency of review	Questions
Vision and values Mission statement	Every few years or so – should provide a long-term purpose for the project	Are we still needed? What has changed? Do our vision and values guide all that we do?
The project's success criteria	Every few months	Are we likely to achieve our success criteria? What is working? What are the milestones towards success?
The project's strategy and direction	The strategy should be looked at regularly and reformed at least annually	Are we doing the right things? How can we make the best impact? What is happening in our environment? What should our direction and priorities be? What should stay the same and what should change?
The project's specific objectives and workplan	The specific plan should be agreed at least annually and monitored monthly	How do we implement our strategy? Are we on time and within budget? What else is happening? Are our outputs making an impact?
The project's critical success factors	The list of internal factors which have to work for the project to be effective. They should be agreed at least annually and reviewed regularly	Where are the internal blocks What stops us being effective? How are we managing the critical success factors?

It very important for a project to take time to review progress and learn from its first year or two. The review process needs to be built in to staff meetings, committee meetings and planning sessions. It should give the project staff a chance to evaluate what they are doing, compare it with what the project was expected to do and plan the next stages

The changing role of the management committee

Projects that have management committees or boards to govern and oversee their work need to consider how the committee's role changes during the first year or so. It is likely that committee members' individual and collective contribution will have been crucial in the period leading up to the project's establishment. They will have nurtured the idea, developed the project plan and secured the resources to turn it into reality. As the project starts operating, the committee's role becomes less certain. Staff start to set the tone and pace. Things need to happen too quickly for committee members to be fully informed of developments. They can very easily lose control. The committee can start to feel inactive or even redundant.

It is possible to look at how the committee develops as it moves through four stages:

Stage 1

The committee is highly active. It is involved with all the day to day activity of the project. Its members carry out work and play a crucial role in getting the project established.

Stage 4

The committee steers. It is concerned with the long-term direction of the project. It develops strategy, evaluates work and makes sure the project keeps a vision.

Stage 2

The committee works with paid staff who take on an increasingly active role. The committee acts as a sounding board and supports the staff.

Stage 3

The committee acts as a rubber stamp. It approves decisions taken by the staff. It has little direct influence on what happens. Its role is mainly ceremonial.

In stage one, without the active contribution of the committee the project would not happen. Often in this stage there are no paid staff so the committee has to do the work.

Stage two can last for some time. The staff and committee find a way of communicating and keeping each other in touch. Over time the staff take on more responsibility and the committee's role becomes more 'backseat' or passive.

In stage three the committee only approves the decisions presented to it by the staff or makes decisions of major importance such as hiring and firings. It has little direct involvement in the project. Often the committee is composed of people who have been invited on to it to give the project credibility.

In stage four the committee is more concerned with directing than with day to day management. It ensures that the project has a strategy that will help it towards its vision and that the project regularly evaluates its performance. Matters of operational detail are delegated to paid staff.

Overstaying your welcome

Anyone who knew Pengor Arts Centre would agree that Martin had been central to setting it up. It was his idea. He had built support for it, found the building and navigated the project through a complicated obstacle course of planning applications and funding bids. He had chaired the committee from the start, but had taken on a whole host of other roles, from spokesman to caretaker. In the three months between the Centre opening and the new Director starting he had acted as unpaid Director. Quite often it had looked as if the Centre would not get off the ground. It was, everyone agreed, a tribute to Martin's vision and energy over three years that it had.

Sam, the new Director, found the Centre in good shape. She was new to the area so Martin made a real effort to help her to settle in. They worked well together. He had plenty of ideas and contacts. She had many of the managerial and financial skills needed to get the Centre into shape. She decided to spend the first few months getting the Centre organised. Several issues, such as proper budget systems and basic health and safety issues had been neglected in the rush to get the Centre going.

In retrospect tensions between Sam and Martin were obvious at the second management board meeting. Sam presented two papers. The first set out a new budget. The current budget had unrealistic income predictions. Savings would have to be made, some projects might have to be delayed. The second paper called for a reduced programme of events. There was a danger, she argued, of doing too many things badly. It was better to do a few things effectively in the first year and then build up. Martin hurried the discussion through. Although the papers were agreed he showed no enthusiasm for them. In the pub afterwards, he joked about how the bureaucrats had taken over.

Three months later the treasurer met Sam at a Christmas party. Sam had now spent seven months in the job. She said that the 'honeymoon period was well and truly over'. When pressed she explained that Martin carried on regardless. She reckoned that every week he had at least three ideas about what the Centre could do. He regularly made commitments on the Centre's behalf without telling Sam. He ignored the perilous financial situation by arguing that money always turned up for good ideas. Sam respected Martin a great deal. She just felt stifled by him.

The treasurer talked to Martin about the situation. He admitted to feeling frustrated. He genuinely supported and understood what Sam was doing. But it just was not fun any more! Setting up the Centre and getting it going had been exciting. Running it was not.

Over the holiday Martin thought about his position. In January he shocked everyone by resigning from the committee. He could not see any way that he could scale down his involvement. He did not want to be involved only on the fringes of the Centre. He realised that it was time for him to move on.

It was with a genuine feeling of regret that the committee accepted Martin's decision. Sam did feel a sense of loss, but felt that she could now do what she was paid for without being blocked.

This raises several issues about the role of the founder in a project:

■ Is there a point in the project's development when the founder or original visionary needs to allow others to take over? Can they be so central to everything that they block other people's development and growth?

■ Are some people better at setting projects up and being innovative rather than in managing projects?

■ What structures and processes are needed in a project to review the type of management needed at a given time? How do you stop relationships breaking down? How do you review people's different contribution?

Six months later Martin was busy launching a youth project. He was full of energy and enthusiasm for it. But this time he planned to start it, hand it over and then move on.

All these stages have their positive and negative side. In stage one the contribution of volunteer committee members is crucial. More often than not they do the work. But they need to give up these tasks as the project takes on staff. This is often a cause of conflict as committee members try to hang on to things they enjoy.

In stage two the partnership can work well provided there is a clear agreement about expectations, responsibilities and delegation. In this stage there is often confusion about what can be decided by the staff and what they need to take to the committee. It is not at all unusual to find committees having long debates on minor items of expenditure while major decisions relating to the project's long-term future go through without discussion.

Many management committees operate at stage three. They claim to have an arm's length relationship with the project and insist that it is not their role to meddle in the day to day workings. They are there to lend authority, support and guidance when needed, although they can often become remote and know little about what is really happening. They are too out of touch to operate good governance.

In stage four, the committee is often able to help the project staff see the bigger picture, by encouraging evaluation, measuring progress and keeping the project in line with its vision. To do this well requires considerable skill, good information and a 'feel' for project's style and culture. Often, as a committee moves through the four stages, some members fall away or are reluctant to move on. Several projects have had to find ways of managing round their committee.

Managing the change

The following points are possible strategies for helping committees to move on and develop alongside the project.

Encourage committee review sessions

Encourage the committee to review its performance and role regularly – at least annually. In one project the management board reviews its effectiveness every four months at the end of its business meeting. It works through five questions:

- What have we as a committee added to the project?
- What should we need more of?
- What should we do need less of?
- What are the main issues we need to focus on?
- Are we keeping to our business plan?

Run a skills audit

Encourage the committee to review its membership and skills regularly. Several organisations now use skills audits to encourage committees to review their membership and identify any gaps. The usual method is for the committee to identify the skills and knowledge needed to govern the organisation effectively and then identify gaps in the committee's membership.

Stress responsibilities

Be clear about what is expected of committee members. Charity law places an obligation on trustees always to act in the best interest of the charity. This means that committee members are expected to put the organisation's needs and interests before their own first (something co-opted members in particular sometimes find hard to come to terms with).

Agree expectations

Some organisations produce a job description for the committee setting out minimum requirements and obligations. Others agree how much time committee members should expect to give to the project each month. If committee members regularly go over this time it probably means that they are either meeting too much, are too involved in day to day matters or that the project is in crisis.

Manage information

Regularly review the committee's information needs. Committees often get too much or too little. They are either swamped with reports and papers or are kept in the dark. The flow of information between staff and committee needs to be negotiated and agreed. The information the committee needs to keep itself informed, exercise its responsibilities and contribute to the project's long-term direction must be identified.

Train and support committee members

It is common for committee members to be closely in touch in the early days of a project, but to lose touch with new developments. Often so much is happening in a particular organisation, field or sector that it is very hard to keep up to date.

One committee member described how she realised that she was out of touch with her project. 'We are involved in special needs housing. I am an accountant so I was lined up to chair the finance sub committee. Housing finance in general, and special needs finance in particular, change rapidly. Often in discussions I realised that I was out of date. I was concerned that my slowness could block the project's development. To keep up to date with developments would be a full-time job. I do not need to know and indeed probably should not know the detail. That's why we have a finance officer. What I do need to know is the general picture and the right questions to ask. We now have a training budget for the committee. We use it for attending courses and briefings externally and for running three in house committee briefings a year.'

Encourage the committee to have a 'helicopter vision'

Effective committees can make a unique contribution to a project. They should understand the project's purpose and values. Yet they are not part of it on a day to day or week to week basis. They should be able to operate a helicopter vision by 'rising above the day to day detail and helping the project to take a broader view of what is happening'. They need to help the project by ensuring that the direction is not lost and occasionally helping the project stand back from the activity and take a fresh look at itself.

Moving the project on

The project's journey from being a new entity to its mainstream phase needs careful thought. Often projects are launched with tremendous enthusiasm and confidence. There is a lot of energy and willingness to experiment. But at some stage it needs to move on. It needs to establish a pattern of work that is sustainable and realistic.

A health project experienced considerable 'growing pains' in moving from being a new project to being a mainstream one. Its first two years had been full of innovation and experimentation. It developed a series of health programmes that were very popular and broke new ground. Considerable staff time went into programme development and design. Towards the end of the second year negotiations started with local health and social care authorities for two to three year service contracts. The purchasing authorities were very keen on the project, but 'needed to see numbers'. They wanted to have significantly more programmes, with a minimum of ten participants. In the first two years the project had rarely ever run the same programme twice. It constantly redesigned, evaluated and developed its product. It took a considerable effort of will to move from developing the prototype to moving into service production. One of the project workers talked about how:

'We wanted to keep improving the prototype, but really that was unrealistic. We had to find a way of delivering the programme in a way that was cost effective and efficient. We had to move the project on. We did not want to move away from our research and design activities. We were inclined to be perfectionists. But the reality was that we had to find a way of making the programme viable and to show that it could be delivered.'

The following issues need planning and managing.

Consolidating the project

After its start-up phase a project needs to change pace. It needs to develop effective ways of organising its work and maintaining relationships, both internally and externally. Project staff should spend some time developing processes and systems that enable and support the project's work. Teams and committees need training and support to help them work well. External partners, backers and contacts need to be worked with to sustain and develop their goodwill. People often resist consolidation. Doing new things, making new plans and developing new relations often seem much more exciting.

Identifying and building on early successes

Success creates more success. All too often in not-for-profit organisations successes are ignored and not acknowledged. One experienced public sector worker described how she only found out about her good work and successes at her leaving party. In projects it is useful to look for and celebrate early examples of the project making a successful impact. This can help encourage other successes, create a positive atmosphere and make people feel that their past and current contribution was worthwhile.

Exercise – Mid-point review

Past

Looking back at the original project idea:

- Do any aspects need rethinking?
- Do any elements of the original idea need rethinking?
- Do any original assumptions need challenging?

What have we learnt since the project started?

If we were starting this project today what would we do differently?

Present

What works?

What is not working well?

What needs attention?

Future

Are there any aspects of the project's plan that need changing or rethinking?

What kind of succession or exit strategy might be possible?

What action should come out of this review?

King Street Development Project mid-point review

The King Street Development Project was set up to support the development of strong and sustainable community groups. The project's two staff offered a range of services including training, advice, feasibility studies and practical help, to a range of developing and established community groups. After the project's first nine months the staff and management board completed this mid-point review:

Past

Looking back at the original project idea:

Do any aspects need rethinking?
Do any elements of the original idea need rethinking?
Do any original assumptions need challenging?

- There is a strong demand for our work.
- The original assumption was that the service must be free – some groups have the resources to pay or can tap into special funding.

What have we learnt since the project started?

- That the development process takes longer than we thought. It can take up to two years to get a new group up and running.
- We have focused on technical and management support such as finance and constitutional issues, they are important, but miss other issues such as vision and leadership.

If we were starting this project today what would we do differently?

- Work in more depth with fewer groups.
- Explore ways in which we can get groups to learn from each other.
- Stress the importance of having a shared vision.

Present

What works?

- One to one advice work
- Funding workshops
- Resource centre

What is not working well?

- Full day training courses have not recruited well.
- Have not been able to do outreach work with groups that are usually neglected.

What needs attention?

- Training plan
- Project's targets

Future

Are there any aspects of the project's plan that need changing or rethinking?

- Need to agree priorities.
- How should we determine which groups get most support?

What kind of succession or exit strategy might be possible?

- Explore possibility of some services generating income.
- Identify possible alternative funders.

What action should come out of this review?

- Committee to discuss:
  - priorities
  - future of training
  - what happens when our funding ends.

The danger of complacency

It is very easy to become complacent once a project has started working. It is tempting to fall into routines, stop thinking and start driving on 'automatic pilot'. The project does something because 'we have always done it that way'. Regular evaluation sessions, contact with outside agencies, a commitment to learning, the involvement of new people and a constant curiosity can overcome complacency.

The possibility of the project being bounced into other things

New opportunities can emerge or circumstances can change. These opportunities and changes have to be balanced against the project's agreed strategy and plan.

Managing changes to the plan

A refusal to think about change by rigidly sticking to the original idea will probably be perilous. On the other hand, continually adjusting and altering the project will probably mean that it will lose its cohesion, identity and original vision and values. Any changes should be made in an explicit way by rewriting the original project strategy and success criteria rather than incorporating them by absorption.

Further growth

If a project is developing well it is tempting to think about expansion beyond its original base. Projects may choose to expand in size, in geography or in scope. Growth can be very exciting. But planned badly it can also cause problems. It can lead to uneven development, put strain on the organisation, pull resources out of the existing activities and reduce the sharpness of the project's original focus. Growth needs to be thought through. What is the project's optimum size (i.e. when it is able to do what it wants to do most effectively)? Can one successful project's lessons and circumstances be replicated?

Should the project aim to become permanent?

Often fixed-term projects aspire to becoming permanent organisations. In many ways this is understandable. But some projects are successful because they are *not* permanent. They are focused and build up energy because their time is limited. Such success factors are often difficult to transfer into a permanent organisation. Sometimes it is more effective to spend time early in the project's life developing strategies that will enable its work to be taken up by others on a longer-term basis, rather than chasing long-term funding.

The project's life cycle

Projects seem to have a certain ecology. They can develop and grow fast, they reach a peak and then a plateau. Unless something changes (or the project closes) the project can drift into decline. The original energy and direction that set it up can easily (and sometimes quickly) drift away. Regular reviews, creative thinking and good strategic management can help monitor where you are on the project's life cycle. This helps to plan for and think about what comes next.

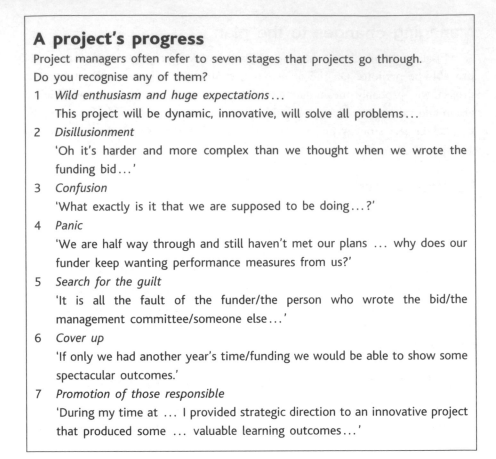

A project's progress

Project managers often refer to seven stages that projects go through. Do you recognise any of them?

1   *Wild enthusiasm and huge expectations...*
    This project will be dynamic, innovative, will solve all problems...

2   *Disillusionment*
    'Oh it's harder and more complex than we thought when we wrote the funding bid...'

3   *Confusion*
    'What exactly is it that we are supposed to be doing...?'

4   *Panic*
    'We are half way through and still haven't met our plans ... why does our funder keep wanting performance measures from us?'

5   *Search for the guilt*
    'It is all the fault of the funder/the person who wrote the bid/the management committee/someone else...'

6   *Cover up*
    'If only we had another year's time/funding we would be able to show some spectacular outcomes.'

7   *Promotion of those responsible*
    'During my time at ... I provided strategic direction to an innovative project that produced some ... valuable learning outcomes...'

Managing the project's closure

Winding up a project can be difficult. Often people connected to the project do not want it to end – they have come to depend on it or had hoped that it might continue. Increasingly managers are having to deal with closure and endings. Here are six ideas drawn from experience:

- **Keep the end date firmly in mind.** Plan the project's critical path (see chapter 8) so that the end date is a central focus. Make sure the project does not simply fade away. Use exit strategies to ensure that the end is carefully planned for and managed.

- **Use and develop the project's network.** If appropriate build a network of people who can help carry the work on after the project has ceased. Keep them informed and involved.

- **Be willing to hand things over.** Organise a gradual programme of advance briefings, consultations and training to enable other people to take on the project's work. Pilot exercises, resource materials, handbooks, contact points, follow up meetings, on-site consultancy and user networks can help.

■ **Look after the project team.** Acknowledge possible feelings of loss. A key issue is in helping people to move on to other roles and projects. A useful approach is to identify and record individual and group successes.

■ **Record learning.** A useful exercise is to pull together the key lessons learnt by people working on the project. As well as contributing to the project's evaluation, this can also help in follow-on activities and other projects.

■ **Celebrate – end on a high.** Aim to end the project on some kind of high. A conference to share the project's work, a publication or even just a good party can help people who have played a role feel that their contribution has been worthwhile and has been recognised. Ending on a positive note can create goodwill towards follow on projects and activities.

Ten reasons to close a project down

1   It has achieved its purpose/mission.
2   Other people do the same thing better.
3   The project's output is not worth the input.
4   The original assumptions, needs and driving forces behind the project have changed significantly.
5   The only purpose served by going on would be to continue to exist as an organisation.
6   The project is persistently dogged by internal conflicts and disputes that stop work from being done.
7   It has fundamentally lost its users' and backers' confidence.
8   It is no longer financially viable.
9   Its resources could be used to much greater effect elsewhere.
10 Any of the above, plus the lack of enough people inside and outside the project committed to turning it round.

Green City Centre

Green City Centre's management committee had been very keen to take on a three-year two-worker project to encourage people to volunteer to take part in environmental initiatives.

Green City's Director explained to the committee that, although the project would be technically part of the Centre, it would enjoy some independence. As Director she would supervise and support the project workers and the

Centre would look after the project's payroll, accounting and administration. For this the Centre would receive an annual management fee of £12,000 (14 per cent of the project's annual budget).

For the first few months things seemed to go well. The project workers relied heavily on Green City's staff to develop contacts and to identify potential volunteers and volunteering opportunities. The project enjoyed a 'honeymoon period'. The staff worked hard. The project received some very good local and regional publicity and was even featured in a government publication as an example of 'innovative good practice'. The project workers established an advisory group of local environmental activists to help shape the project's plan and to provide feedback and support.

Mid-way through the second year Green City's Director tabled a special item at the Centre's management committee. She explained that she was becoming increasingly concerned about the relationship between the Centre and the project. She identified four issues:

- **A style clash.** The Green City Centre had committed itself to bringing environmental issues into the mainstream. She was concerned that the project workers seemed to prefer to work with a few dedicated environmental activists rather than the general public. She felt the project could damage the Centre's strong public image.
- **Potential competition for future funding.** She was concerned that the project workers and some of the advisory group were planning to make bids to secure future funding, some of which would be to the same funders that Green City was planning to approach.
- **Organisational conflicts.** The Centre's office manager had complained that the project workers made regular and at times unreasonable demands for office support. There had been instances where the project workers had ignored the Centre's administrative procedures and when challenged they had claimed that the procedures did not apply to them. The office manager claimed that the project was proving to be expensive to administer, as resources often leaked from the Centre to the project.
- **A management clash.** The project advisory group had started to behave more like a management committee. At its last meeting it had agreed that one of the project workers could attend a conference, despite there being no money in the budget for such an event. It had also asked for a report on the project's budget and queried whether the management payment to the Centre represented 'good value'.

The management committee decided to ask two of its members to work with the Director to resolve these issues. Over the next three months the group did four things that resolved the situation and reduced conflict:

1   It drafted a policy statement setting out the relationship between the Centre and the project. This clarified the role of the advisory group as being to advise on the future development of the work, but not to manage or direct the project's resources. It was agreed that the advisory group should be treated as a standing sub committee of the Centre's management committee.

2   It convened a planning session with the project staff, some of the advisory group and some of the Centre's staff to look at areas of co-operation and how the project's work fitted into the Centre's overall mission and strategy.

3   It arranged for the office manager to carry out a monitoring exercise to establish the actual cost of housing the project. This simple exercise measured the Centre's input into the project and the use by the project of the Centre's resources.

4   It spent some time looking at options for the project. They identified three possibilities:
    ■   The project could work to become an independent body, with its own staff and funding, and leave the Centre.
    ■   It could stay part of the Centre, but have an independent identity and profile.
    ■   The Centre could seek funds to carry on the work of the project at a reduced level once its current funding had ceased. The project's work would become a mainstream part of the Centre.

The group suggested that all the options needed testing and evaluating, with a view to making a clear decision at least a year before the project's current funding ended so that alternative funding bids could be made.

Key management issues checklist

Has your project:

☐   Planned a schedule of project reviews to keep the project on track?

☐   Agreed the role that any management committee should play?

☐   Planned how to support the project's staff in the lead up to the project's closure?

☐   Planned the project's closure in a positive way?

MEASURING UP

This chapter looks at:

- Reasons for monitoring and evaluation
- Definitions
- Developing and using performance measures and indicators
- Approaches to project evaluation
- Making evaluation work

Over the past ten years there has been considerable interest in how organisations measure, monitor and evaluate their work. A whole range of performance measures and indicators, reviews and studies have been developed in the public sector.

> The director of one agency described measurement overload:
>
> *'I sometimes feel that we are sinking under the weight of all these systems. I think that we will soon reach the stage where for each person working we will need to have another person monitoring and reporting on their work!'*

Reasons for monitoring and evaluation

It is useful to look at why projects need to spend time on monitoring and evaluation. The driving forces behind monitoring and evaluation can be divided into two categories – accountability and learning and development.

Accountability

There are a number of reasons why projects need to be accountable.

Funders and sponsors expect it

In the public sector politicians and managers expect regular information about the performance of projects they have commissioned or funded. It is not enough to be doing good work – it needs to be proved.

The need to show and test value for money

The government has a strong interest in value for money and best value to show that public spending is used wisely and properly.

Measurement as a key part of the contracting process

Funding systems are moving from a grant aid process to using contracts and service agreements that set out clear expectations of what the project will do. Most agreements set out the process for monitoring and evaluation. Performance measures are used to judge performance and delivery.

Sponsors need to show results

Often sponsors and funders need to show that they are making an impact and achieving objectives. Simply showing how much money they have spent is no longer good enough.

Greater public scrutiny

Projects need to be able to produce evidence of their effectiveness to withstand an ever increasing range of value for money studies, spending reviews and policy reviews.

Learning and development

Learning and development are also necessary for a number of reasons.

To find out what works

Good evaluation can help a project learn by identifying what works. It can identify the impact of a project's work and analyse which aspects are effective and which need attention.

To measure achievements

Monitoring and evaluation should show the progress a project is making. This can help the project to focus on its achievements and successes and demonstrate its success to funders, sponsors and others.

To develop understanding

All too often project staff are so heavily involved in working on the project that they lack time to stand back and take a broader view. Good systems encourage people involved in the project to look at trends, identify patterns and improve their practice.

To get feedback from users

Monitoring and evaluation can be an opportunity to open up communication with a project's users. Early feedback can be valuable in developing future plans and identifying any problems.

To link into planning

There should be a strong link between project monitoring and evaluation and project planning. The results of evaluation should inform future plans and shape strategies.

Getting a balance between accountability and learning can be difficult. Some funding bodies appear to be interested only in data and number crunching and not in the broader patterns and longer term impact.

The coordinator of a employment project described how she tackled her funder's narrowness.

'Our main funder seems to love number crunching. It is forever asking for statistics so that it can produce charts and graphs that are really quite meaningless. All they really show is how busy we are. We took a decision to continue to give the funder whatever data it asked for, but we have also have a campaign of trying to show it the effectiveness of our work in ways that cannot be represented on a spreadsheet. We have run presentations to the board to report on key developments. We have also provided case studies showing the longer term outcome of our work. The process of educating our funder has been a long one, but it is starting to pay off.'

Definitions

There is a whole language around monitoring and evaluation. Often the terms are not clearly defined or explained by those that promote, require or use them. Here are some of the main concepts and techniques.

Performance

Performance is what gets done and what happens in a specific time. Performance measures usually focus on the project's 'deliverables'. Examples include the number of users who receive a service or the number or volume of services delivered.

Performance measures and performance indicators

The terms 'measures' and 'indicators' often mean the same thing. They record specific elements of a project's performance. For example, a community arts project might have one measure to record the number of groups it works with and another measure to record the number of people participating in the project.

Quality assurance and quality standards

Standards are agreed statements of the minimum level of service that people should be able to expect from an organisation. For example, an advice project might have minimum standards for confidentiality, record keeping, casework and internal management processes. Good quality standards should ensure that an organisation works in a consistent way. Quality assurance is the process of developing, managing and monitoring the application of standards. Externally awarded systems that validate an organisation's management of standards include IS9000 and PQASSO (Practical Quality Assurance System for Smaller Organisations).

Value for money

In the public sector a value for money review should look at a project to ensure that it provides a good return for the money invested in it. A value for money approach is constructed around three approaches:

- Is it *economic*? Does the level of resources allocated make good economic sense? How does the cost of the activity compare with other projects or alternatives?
- Is it *efficient*? Is the output sufficient? If the activity was better organised could more outputs be delivered for the same (or less) input?
- Is it *effective*? Does it work? Did it meet the original objectives? Are the outcomes worth the input?

Best value

Best value is a public sector review process whereby a public authority should look at how it organises a service or function to ensure that it provides best value. A best value review should compare the costs involved in a particular service with alternatives, challenge the basis on which the service is currently provided and consult with users and the community on their view of the service.

Developing and using performance measures and indicators

A project needs to develop its own performance measures and encourage project funders and sponsors to use them rather than have inappropriate or irrelevant measures imposed on them.

A checklist for using performance measures

The following points provide a useful checklist for agreeing and reviewing measures.

Are the measures:

■ Related to the project's aims and plan?
Do they link back to the overall aims, strategy and specific plans set out in the project's plan?

■ Agreed in advance?
Performance measures should not be imposed retrospectively.
The choice of measures and the measurement method should be agreed at the start of the project.

■ Capable of being managed or improved?
Is what is being measured determined by the performance of the project? For example, a voluntary group working with young homeless people is not responsible for the numbers of homeless young people in its area (in fact its work might establish that there are more young homeless people than previously estimated). The numbers of young homeless people in a town is an indicator of social needs and social trends, and not an indicator of performance.

■ Easy to collect?
Is the method of recording performance easy to use? Measurement systems should be integrated into the project's procedures such as booking systems, casework record systems or diaries rather than the project staff having to fill in separate monitoring systems.

- Measurable?
  Are some aspects of the project's work particularly difficult to measure? Or would the costs or time involved in collecting data be too much? Could there be objections to the process of collecting information or might it cause suspicion amongst clients or users?
- Easy to understand?
  When collated and analysed does the information give a clear and unambiguous picture of what is happening in the project? Does the measurement system allow space for trends and changes in performance to be explained?
- Reflecting an even and total picture?
  The measurement system should report on all aspects of the project's activity, not just those elements that are easier to get information about.
- Linked into planning?
  Is there a clear link back into the project's future planning systems? Are trends in performance used to develop future strategies and workplans?
- Related to the project's values?
  Does the measurement system take into account the ethos and values that should underpin and inform the project's work? For example, an education project had a strong commitment to working with people who were traditionally excluded from post-school education. Its first set of performance measures concentrated on student numbers. They indicated that recruiting a high volume of students was what mattered. The project revised these measures to take account of its effectiveness in recruiting students from key priority groups.
- Cost effective?
  How much will it cost to record and collect the information? How much staff time will it take up? Is the value of collecting information about performance worth the cost and time involved?

Designing measures

A simple guide for developing performance measures is based around five stages.

What is the project's overall aim?

The work carried out in the project's definition stage should have clarified the intended outcomes and success criteria. The measures used should relate to these aims. The use of good measurement systems can help to make the aims feel more achievable and more tangible. If an aim cannot be measured than how will you know if you have achieved it or are even making any impact on it?

What values should influence the project?

All measures should be informed by the project's values. For example, a project might have agreed a commitment to work with the most isolated and excluded clients. Simply recording the number of clients might not take into account the type of client.

What do we want to measure?

The project needs to agree which key elements of its work need measuring. It needs to develop a range of realistic measures that give a good view of the project's development and report on those issues most important to key stakeholders. It is useful to ask people what they would find useful to know about the project's performance.

What are the possible measures and indicators?

After listing what is to be measured, the next stage is to decide upon the most appropriate and cost efficient method of collecting the required information. The four level approach (see below) is a useful tool.

How will the information be used and interpreted?

How will the measures be used? Who will see them? It is often worthwhile to think how the project can help people to understand the information. Raw data on its own is often misleading. The project needs to be able to present the information in a way that explains the background, context and trends that might have affected performance.

Measuring at four levels

A practical way of deciding what measures to use is to structure the measurement process at four levels.

1 The project's activity/deliverables

Measures report on what the project has been doing. They are focused on the project's outputs and record the tangible work of the project.

2 Reaction and feedback

Measures at this level report on what key stakeholders think about the project's activities. Are there any complaints or negative reactions? What positive feedback or praise has the project picked up?

3 Impact

Impact is what happens in the short term as a result of the output. Impacts are steps towards the desired outcomes.

4 Outcomes

Outcomes are the results of the project. They can be about what has changed for the user or the community as a result of the project. Outcome measurement needs time, to see that the project has a lasting impact and not simply a short-term result.

Approaches to project evaluation

Project evaluation often sounds more complex than it is or needs to be. Evaluation should be focused on four questions:

- Has the project achieved its original aims and purpose?
- Has it been a success?
- What can be learnt from the project?
- What new needs and issues might emerge as a result of the project?

Effective evaluation needs to be linked to the project's definition and planning stage. The project's evaluation should not be an afterthought, hurriedly thrown together at the end of the project. It needs to build on the work carried out in the definition and planning stages and the information collected as the project starts to deliver.

Measuring a project at four levels

An economic development project developed a measurement structure for monitoring its work on advising, helping and supporting individuals setting up small and medium sized businesses in a local estate.

The project's activity/deliverables

Measure	Method
Number of enquiries	Reception records
Number of advice sessions	Diaries
Number of training courses delivered	Training records
Number of consultancies undertaken	Consultant's records

Reaction and feedback

Measure	Method
Client satisfaction	Postal surveys after courses and advice sessions
	Six-monthly client meetings led by independent recorder
Feedback from clients	Recording complaints and compliments

Impact

Measure	Method
Clients taking appropriate action to take their business idea forward	Number of viable business plans produced
Business start ups	Quarterly contact with clients

Outcomes

Measure	Method
Businesses successful 18 months after start up	Follow up phone contact with clients
Businesses having positive impact on the local economy – jobs created – annual turnover – business spend in the local community	Follow up survey of ex-clients after six months

Exercise – Measuring a project at four levels

Identify the important measures for your project at four levels:

The project's activity/deliverables

Measure   *Method*

Reaction and feedback

Measure   *Method*

The project's activity/deliverables

Measure   *Method*

The project's activity/deliverables

Measure   *Method*

> ## Watch out for side effects
>
> Often the most useful outcomes are what happens alongside a project. A good evaluation process should also pick up side effects.
>
> A community drugs project spent a year working with young people on an estate. The project measured its work in terms of how many young people it worked with, the number of families supported, number of awareness sessions delivered and so on.
>
> Towards the end of the project it was pointed out that the way the project was working was different from other initiatives. The project had convened a partnership group to advise and support the project. The group was made up of representatives from the main local agencies – neighbourhood police officer, doctors, head teacher, youth worker and social services. Because of the project leader's skilled facilitation the group had been a success. For the first time ever people had worked together and shared experiences. In fact the group had agreed to continue working together after the project had ended.
>
> Although not deliberately set out in the project's plan this represented a significant positive outcome.

Much of the literature about evaluation talks about two types: process and programme.

Process evaluation

Process evaluation is focused on how the project works and is organised. It looks at the ways the project uses or used its resources and the effectiveness of the project's systems for planning, communication and managing. Process evaluation is usually geared at the project's internal structure and life. Issues might include:

- Could we work better?
- Did people feel involved in the project?
- How well does the project communicate?

> ## A useful measure
> One useful measure is how much time the project spends on measuring and evaluating its performance. Is the time invested worthwhile? Does all the measurement and monitoring make any real difference?

Programme evaluation

Programme evaluation aims to measure the impact and lasting change the project has made on the original need. It is focused on the impact that the project has had on the user and should look at the project's outputs and outcomes. Issues might include:

- Is the project making a difference?
- Has it met the identified need – has the need changed?
- What have been the outcomes?

Output measures	Outcome measures
Volume	Did the output create change?
Numbers taking part	Did the benefits last?
Income raised	What impact are we making?
Activities	How are we affecting needs?
Services delivered	What is happening as a result of our work?

Designing a project evaluation

Why are we doing it?

You need to be clear about why the project is being evaluated. What will the evaluation be used for? Who will own it – is the evaluation being carried out for the project or host agency, or for the project sponsor or funder?

What do we want to know?

Evaluation reports often cover too many issues and so lack a clear focus. A project evaluation can focus on:

- **Process or programme issues** – should it be about how the project is organised or about its impact and effectiveness?
- **Revisiting the original idea and assumptions** – the evaluation can test the ideas and thinking that underpinned the project's definition stage. Did the project fully understand what was needed? With the benefit of experience what would we do differently?
- **Feedback** – the evaluation can collect stakeholders' views and opinions. What do they think of it? How do they feel it compares with other initiatives?

Who should do the evaluation?

The evaluation can be carried out by project workers, or external evaluators can be commissioned. There are advantages and disadvantages of both approaches. Evaluation carried out by people working on or strongly connected with the project may lack independence and objectiveness. However, there may be more chance of the project acting on the issues they identify. External evaluators should bring a level of independence and impartiality – they should not have a particular stake in the evaluation's outcome. Their independence might also bring credibility to the evaluation. But external evaluators are not cheap – their cost needs to be built into the project's budget – and they need to understand the idea, ethos and values that hold the project together. Sometimes using an external evaluator might cause anxiety amongst project staff. They might feel that the evaluation is being 'done to them' rather than being a shared learning experience.

One possibility is to use a mixture of external and internal evaluation. One project established an evaluation team made up of staff and committee members. They also appointed an external consultant to work with the team. The team carried out surveys, ran interviews and focus groups and visited similar projects. The consultant advised on the process, developed the methodology, carried out interviews when the team felt people would talk more easily to an external person, and facilitated a team session to produce the evaluation report.

How should we do it?

A simple process for project evaluations involves eight stages.

1 Establish the issues

- Why are we doing it – for our learning and development or for accountability?
- What do we need to evaluate? What are the key issues we want to find out about?

2 Plan the evaluation

- Who should do it – internal or external evaluator or a mix?
- When should we do it?
- What sort of timetable do we need?

3 Organise the evaluation

- Write a brief setting out the desired outcomes.
- Appoint and brief the evaluation team.
- Agree who needs to be involved.

4 Gather the information

- Use a variety of means – interviews, focus groups, analysis of information, comparisons with similar projects, surveys and questionnaires.

5 Analyse and interpret the information

- Collate the data.
- Identify key conclusions and learning points.
- Draft an evaluation report.

6 Report back

- Discuss the findings within the project and with key stakeholders.
- Identify key issues needing attention.

7 Agree an action plan

- Draft an action plan with short, medium and longer-term action points for the project, the host agency and the sponsor.
- Negotiate the action plan with key stakeholders.

8 Share the evaluation findings

- Disseminate the evaluation findings to interested parties through seminars, meetings and circulation of the report.

Making evaluation work

There are six factors for an effective project evaluation.

Clarity of purpose and ownership

Everyone involved needs to understand why the project is being evaluated and how the evaluation will help to strengthen the project and its work.

A clear set of aims, values and success criteria

The project definition stage needs to have produced and recorded a set of aims, values and success criteria that can be used as a benchmark for the evaluation process. The absence of clear definition or vagueness in definition ('the project aims to lots of good things for lots of people...') makes effective evaluation very difficult as it has nothing against which to measure progress.

Openness and willingness to learn

There needs to be an atmosphere in and around the project in which people feel open to being challenged, are willing to consider feedback and are prepared to learn. It is important that the evaluation is not seen as a 'fault finding' exercise, but rather as a genuine attempt to measure progress, identify successes and move the project forward.

Involvement in the process

Experience suggests that if people are involved in designing the evaluation process and identifying the issues to be evaluated and are kept in touch with the process they are more likely to feel inclined to learn and change. If an element of secrecy dominates the process and a final report is dropped on people it is possible they will feel disconnected from the exercise and be unwilling to give it any serious attention.

A variety of techniques

No single technique works well all the time. Surveys, interviews and focus groups can all be used both well and badly. A single technique can also be over-used. It is better to use a range of techniques to gather information and identify common points and messages.

Clarity about how it will be used

All too often the written report is seen as the main focus of the evaluation. Whilst it is important, you also need to think about how to share the results through events, media coverage and disseminating the findings to key parties. The evaluation report must be clear enough for the project to draw from it specific strategies, plans and actions to take the project forward.

Measures and indicators

All these measures and indicators can be used to measure and report on different aspects of a project's performance.

Type of measure/indicator	Example	Comment
Unit cost The total cost of the project divided by the number of times it is used or by the number of users.	The total cost of a community safety project was £45,000. Over a year the project worked with 182 users. Therefore the unit cost was £247.	Unit costs can give a very raw figure. They only make sense if the 'unit' does not change much and requires the same level of input and time.
Overheads/management costs Amount spent on administration, management and infrastructure costs as opposed to direct delivery costs.	A project was able to show that it only spent 12 per cent of its income on administration and management functions.	Some funders are reluctant to pay for management or administrative costs. You need to show that management costs are reasonable and that the management function adds value to the project.
Take-up rate Data on the number of times the project is used.	A telephone helpline measured the number of callers.	This really only shows how busy the project is – you also need to show quality and effectiveness.

Type of measure/indicator	Example	Comment
Performance against an agreed standard Recording compliance with pre-set standards of minimum practice.	A community care project had standards setting out minimum levels of response times for people needing its services. It monitored performance against the standards.	Often used as part of a quality assurance process to demonstrate that the project works to best practice standards.
Performance against an agreed plan Recording completion of pre-set objectives and plans.	A community development project produced a quarterly report listing progress against the targets and objectives set in the project's workplan.	The plan needs to have some flexibility to allow for unpredictable events and demands.
User feedback Collation of user opinions, reactions and comments.	Recording positive and negative feedback from people who use the project based on complaints, reaction sheets and surveys.	Often hard to get feedback from users. Who collects the information can be an important issue.
Case audits/sample checks Checking that work has been properly carried out.	A health project monitored one in ten cases to ensure that they had been managed in line with agreed policy.	The project must have clear standards of the expected levels of good practice.

Type of measure/indicator	Example	Comment
Follow up reviews A measure of the longer term impact of the project.	An employment project kept in touch with a sample of former trainees to monitor their progress.	Often used to measure outcomes as well as outputs. Can be time consuming and needs good systems to track users once they have moved on from the project.
Matching expectations with experience A comparison of what users expected and what the project delivered.	A training project developed an evaluation programme whereby participants recorded their hopes and expectations. The statements were recorded and used at the end of the project to identify progress and achievements.	Can be useful for measuring people's progress. Need to recognise that needs and expectations change.
Policy measures Recording actions taken to ensure that key policies are implemented.	A project reported on what it had done to put key policies on equality and user involvement into practice.	A useful way of ensuring that policies are not just paper commitments.

Type of measure/indicator	Example	Comment
Referral indicators A measure of the route by which users were referred to the project.	A youth project monitored which agencies were referring young people to the project.	Analysis of referrals can produce useful information on the project's marketing and external relations and the use made of it by other agencies.
No service given A measure of when the project had been unable to provide a service.	A community development project kept a log every time it had to turn down a user – either because the project was at capacity or because the requested service was not in the project's remit.	Often this information is never collected or collated, as people are simply turned away. This measure can help a project identify unmet demands and gaps.
Lost opportunities Recording opportunities missed because the project did not have the capacity to respond.	An opportunity cost happens when a project does not have the resources or time to respond to an opportunity properly. A housing project was unable to become involved in an estate renewal initiative because all staff time was fully committed.	A useful measure to help in future planning and in ensuring that the project is able to respond to new or changing demands.

Measuring up checklist

Has your project:

☐ Planned how the project should be evaluated?

☐ Set aside time and resources for evaluation and monitoring?

☐ Identified relevant measures and indicators to record the project's performance?

☐ Planned how to identify the project's impact and outcomes?

☐ Identified specific issues to be evaluated?

☐ Planned how the information collected will be used?

FURTHER INFORMATION

Publications

Accidental Empires
Robert X Cringely, 1996
ISBN 0 14 025826 4 Addison Wesley/Viking
The brilliantly written story of how the personal computer industry was created 'more or less by accident by amateurs who for the most part still are'

The Complete Guide to Business & Strategic Planning for Voluntary Organisations
Alan Lawrie, 2nd edition 2001 (3rd edition to be published in 2007)
ISBN 1 900360 87 X Directory of Social Change
A detailed guide to putting together a business and strategic plan for voluntary organisations

The Creative Manager
P Evans & R Russell, 1992
ISBN 0 04 440604 5 Unwin Books
A guide to how managers can develop their own problem solving and creative skills

'The Fall and Rise of Strategic Planning', *Harvard Business Review*, January–February, pp107–114
H Mintzberg, 1994
Henry Mintzberg argues that the label 'strategic planning' should be dropped, because stategic planning has impeded strategic thinking

The Fifth Discipline Field book
P Senge, Ross, Smith, Roberts & Kleiner, 1994
ISBN 1 85788 060 9 Nicholas Brealey Publishing
A practical introduction to the development of the idea of a 'learning organisation'

Funding our Future, Core Costs Revisited
ACEVO, 2001
ISBN 1 900685 108 ACEVO
An analysis of the issue of core costs

Innovation and Entrepreneurship
Peter Drucker, 1999
ISBN 0 330 29465 2 Pan Business Books
A look at how businesses can encourage innovation

The Once and Future Pioneers
Stephen Osborne, 1994
ISBN 1 85 449146 6 Joseph Rowntree Foundation
Research report on the extent of innovation within the voluntary organisations

Project Leadership
W Briner, C Geddes & M Hastings, 1996
ISBN 0 556 02794 1 Gower
A practical guide to creating project teams and developing systems for project based organisations

Smart Things to Know about Managing Projects
Donna Deeprose, 2001
ISBN 1 84112 147 Capstone Publishing Ltd
A practical guide to project management

The Sources of Invention
John Jewkes, David Sawers and Richard Stillerman, 1969
Macmillan (out of print)
A frequently cited book about inventors and inventions including more than 50 case histories of important inventions

Superteams: A Blueprint for Organizational Success
Hastings, Bixby & Chaudhry-Lawton, 1986
ISBN 0 00 637049 7 Fontana
An interesting look at how effective teams are developed and encouraged

The Directory of Social Change

The Directory of Social Change (DSC) is an independent voice for positive social change, set up in 1975 to help voluntary organisations become more effective. It does this by providing practical, challenging and affordable information and training to meet the current, emerging and future needs of the sector.

DSC's main activities include:

- researching and publishing reference guides and handbooks;
- providing practical training courses;
- running conferences and briefing sessions;
- organising Charityfair, the biggest annual forum for the sector;
- encouraging voluntary groups to network and share information;
- campaigning to promote the interests of the voluntary sector as a whole.

Contact addresses and telephone numbers can be found at the start of this book, opposite the Contents page.

Books available from DSC

A free booklist containing details of all titles published by DSC can be obtained by contacting the Publications department. Telephone 08450 77 77 07 or e-mail publications@dsc.org.uk for a complete catalogue, or visit the DSC website: www.dsc.org.uk.

Training available from DSC

For a copy of the latest training guide, including details of courses on project management, contact the training department on 08450 77 77 07, e-mail training@dsc.org.uk or visit the DSC website: www.dsc.org.uk.